T0197302

OUT OF THE ORDINARY

OUT OF THE ORDINARY

Ordinary thwarts success.
Out-of-the-Ordinary
changes the world.

MICHAEL BALCH

OUT OF THE ORDINARY
ORDINARY THWARTS SUCCESS. OUT-OF-THE-
ORDINARY CHANGES THE WORLD.

iUniverse books may be ordered through booksellers or by contacting:

iUniverse
1663 Liberty Drive
Bloomington, IN 47403
www.iuniverse.com
1-800-Authors (1-800-288-4677)

ISBN: 978-1-5320-5909-4 (sc)
ISBN: 978-1-5320-5908-7 (hc)
ISBN: 978-1-5320-5910-0 (e)

Library of Congress Control Number: 2018911572

Print information available on the last page.

iUniverse rev. date: 10/16/2018

CONTENTS

CREATIVE EXERCISE

INTRODUCTION

As a person who has spent my life at the intersection of creativity and innovation, I have watched our country's businesses and society stagnate. What do I mean by stagnate? We have become a nation of followers. We have been taught, largely through our educational system to perfect the already known. In school we try to master the standardized tests. The best test takers get the high-profile jobs and help to perfect the processes already in place. Meanwhile, in a country built on ingenuity and hard work, the creative thinkers are dwindling or being muzzled.

Commonplace thinking would lead you to believe some people are highly creative, while others have little to no creativity. That same thinking would also make you believe that some people are born to be leaders and other followers. I am here to say that is false. Everybody is born with creativity. The question is are you encouraging creative thinking, or have you suppressed it to follow the status quo?

Not only will I debug the notion that some people are not born creative, or leaders, but will show you how to become a leader that is creative, innovative, and courageous.

We will learn that a great idea doesn't have to be an off the wall idea to be successful but could come from a minor tweak to a current product, model, or process. We will learn how other successful people found their direction. I will bust myths of who and what an entrepreneur is and what it takes to be one. If you want to better yourself, and the world, this book will guide you through the how's and how not's to being "out-of-the-ordinary" and launch your career into a whole new stratosphere.

BUCKING WHAT YOU KNOW

"Out-of-the-ordinary," or "extraordinary," for that matter connotes something that is of unique or singular character. It can allude to a person who differs from others in an interesting or appealing way or a person of inventive capacity or fresh initiative. Just a few decades ago, psychologists figured out that there are two paths to achievement; "out-of-the-ordinary" and conformity. "Out-of-the-ordinary" is taking the less traveled road, promoting a set of new concepts that initially are very difficult to embrace albeit in the long run they make things better. It is true that nothing is entirely "out-of-the-ordinary" because all ideas derive from one's knowledge of the world. People constantly borrow thoughts, whether inadvertently or intentionally, and are susceptible to 'kleptomnesia,' which is a tendency to remember the ideas of others as one's own accidentally. In this sense, "out-of-the-ordinary" can be explained as involving the introduction and advancement of a relatively unusual idea within a given domain and which has the potential to better that domain.

Out-of-the-ordinary begins with creativity, which involves generating ideas that are both new and useful, but it does not end there. Out-of-the-ordinary persons are those who take the next step of transforming their visions into realities. The founders of Warby Parker, for instance, had the ingenuity to conceptualize an unconventional strategy to sell eyeglasses online and by acting to make them affordable and readily accessible, they became out-of-the-ordinaries (Thayer, 2016). This book is essentially about how one can become more out-of-the-ordinary.

What's in a Browser

A few years back, economist Michael Housman led a project to find out why some customer service agents retained their jobs for more extended periods than others. He collected data from over 30,000 employees who handled calls from banks, cell phone companies, and airlines, suspecting that the histories of their employment would have telltale signals of their commitment. He supposed that persons with histories of job-hopping would opt out sooner, but they did not. In fact, those employees who had stayed in their jobs for the last five years were not any less likely to leave their positions than those who had held five jobs over the past five years. Housman hunted down more hints and found an intriguing correlation between the Internet browser employees used when applying for their jobs and quitting. Employees who used Chrome or Firefox to browse the Web stayed in their jobs 15% longer than those who used Safari or Internet Explorer. Believing this was only a coincidence, Housman conducted a similar analysis for work absences, and the pattern was the same: Safari and Internet Explorer fans were 19% more likely to miss work than Chrome and Firefox users (Grant & Sandberg, 2017).

A further examination of performance involving about three million data points on customer satisfaction, average call length, and sales showed that Chrome and Firefox users had considerably higher sales with shorter call times. Moreover, their clients were more satisfied. Chrome and Firefox users attained client satisfaction levels after three months of work that Safari and Internet Explorer users only attained after four months on the job (Grant & Sandberg, 2017).

Housman noted the browser itself did not cause the employees to retain their jobs, have regular attendance, and succeed. It only indicated critical aspects of their habits. Housman concluded that Chrome and Firefox group were more committed to their jobs and better performers on all metrics because they are more tech savvy. This, however, does not mean that they have more technical knowledge than Safari and Internet Explorer users. On the contrary, the difference came about in how they obtained the browser. Safari and Internet Explorer are default browsers in Windows and Mac computers. These are used by nearly two-thirds of customer service agents who never bother to question whether a better alternative is available. Thus, the act of obtaining Chrome or Firefox demonstrated some resourcefulness on the part of the agent. These agents showed initiative, which though tiny, revealed much about what they could do at work. Those who accepted the defaults of Safari and Internet Explorer approached their jobs in the same fashion. They maintained script in sales calls and adhered to standard operating protocols in dealing with the complaints from customers. They viewed their job descriptions as fixed, thus, when they developed a dissatisfaction, they began to miss days, and eventually quit (The Economist, 2013).

Those who took the initiative to find better browsers, i.e., Chrome and Firefox, took a different approach to their jobs. They sought novel techniques of selling to clients and handling their issues. When they came across any situation that they disliked, they resolved it. Thus, having taken the step to better their circumstances, they were left with little reason to leave. They fashioned the jobs they desired, therefore, becoming the exception, and not the rule (The Economist, 2013).

Likewise, today we live in an "Internet Explorer world." Much of humanity accepts the defaults in life the same way two-thirds of the customer service representatives use default browsers on their computers. In a separate set of provocative studies, a team of psychologists led by John Jost investigated how individuals respond to undesirable default situations. Jost and his team found that people in the highest income bracket were 17% less likely to view economic income inequality as necessary than those in the lowest income bracket. Further, twice as more people in the lowest income bracket than in the highest income bracket were willing to relinquish their freedom of speech if that were necessary to resolve the problems of the United States. The finding that disadvantaged groups consistently back the status quo more than the privileged groups made Jost and his team conclude that those who suffer the most from any given state of affairs paradoxically turn out to be the least likely to challenge, question, change or reject that state of affairs (Jost, Pelham, Sheldon, & Ni Sullivan, 2003).

Jost and his team came up with a theory of system justification to explain this unique phenomenon. The basic idea is that persons are disposed to rationalize the existing state of affairs as legitimate even if it is in direct opposition to their interests. The researchers tracked Republican and Democratic voters before the 2000 presidential elections in the United States and noted that whenever George Bush gained in the polls, he was rated as more desirable by both Republicans and Democrats, with the latter preparing justifications for the expected status quo. The same happened when Al Gore's odds of success rose. Notwithstanding the political ideology, people tended to like a candidate more when his odds of winning rose and less when they dropped. While justifying the default system serves a soothing purpose, acquiescence robs us of the moral outrage to resist injustice. Creative persons will always think of alternative ways of how things should work (Jost et al., 2003).

Thus, the hallmark of out-of-the-ordinary thinking is shunning defaults and probing for better options. It all begins with curiosity, which entails trying to figure out why the default exists in the first place. Persons start questioning defaults when they look at it from a different perspective that gives new insights into old problems. This can be termed as the "vuja de" event, which is the reverse of a déjà vu experience. It was such an event that led to the establishment of the Warby Parker Corporation. The company's founders conjured up the company one night while sitting in a computer lab and pondering over the unreasonable cost of glasses. Until then, they had taken everything for granted, never questioning the status quo.

In fact, David Gilboa, a co-founder, once confessed that he deemed them a medical purchase and so some justification for the price existed. However, after having waited in line at an Apple Store to buy an iPhone, he found himself contrasting the two commodities. Glasses, a crucial aspect of human life for almost a thousand years, had barely changed since their invention. They nonetheless bore a hefty price tag, even costing more than a sophisticated smartphone. These questions led the Warby Parker squad to probe the eyewear industry, and they discovered it was dominated by Luxottica, a European corporation which owned Pearle Vision and LensCrafters, Oakley and Ray-Ban, as well as licenses for Prada and Chanel sunglasses and prescription frames. Luxottica had just made over $7 billion the previous year. With this discovery, the remaining pieces of the puzzle fell into place. There was nothing in the cost of inputs to justify the price. Luxottica was simply capitalizing on its monopoly status to inflate the cost of glasses 20 times over. The default status quo was thus illegitimate; it was merely a decision by a group of persons in a given company. This meant that another group of individuals could make a different choice (Thayer, 2016).

When persons develop curiosity about the dissatisfying defaults in the world, it quickly dawns on them that they are the product of systems and rules that people create. This awareness provides the courage to think of ways to change them. Historian Jean Baker (2006) explains that many women had never given thought to their degraded status as anything but natural before they gained the right to vote. However, as the suffrage movement gained tempo, women began to see that the custom, laws, and religious precepts were, in fact, human-made and thus reversible.

Too Smart for Their Own Good

When psychologists probe the most influential and eminent persons in history, they find that the majority were not unusually gifted as children. Child prodigies, as it often turns out, seldom go on to change the world. Further, most child prodigies do not often outshine their peers from comparable economic backgrounds but who are less precocious all through their lives. This makes sense intuitively. People tend to assume that what gifted kids lack in street smarts they have in book smarts. Thus, since they possess the intellectual chops, they must lack the emotional, practical, and social skills to function well in society. However, closer scrutiny of the evidence shows that this theory is flawed. Less than one-fourth of gifted children have emotional or social problems. Moreover, most of them are well-adjusted (Simonton, 2014).

While child prodigies tend to be rich in both ambition and talent, they cannot move the world forward because they do not learn to go out-of-the-ordinary. They may perform in Carnegie Hall, become champions in chess, and triumph in the science Olympics, but practice merely makes perfection and nothing new is ever created. Gifted kids learn to play beautiful Beethoven symphonies and Mozart melodies, but they never create their own unique scores. All their energy is focused on consuming existing scientific insights rather than producing new ones. They adhere to the set rules of established games instead of investing their own games or rules. All through the way, they win the admiration of their teachers and the approval of their parents (Simonton, 2014).

Research has proven that the most creative kids are least likely to become their teacher's pets. This is because such kids tend to be non-conformists who make their own rules, which leads teachers to discriminate against them and label them troublemakers. In response, most kids, like sheep, fall in line with the programs and keep their out-of-the-ordinary ideas to themselves. In adulthood, most child prodigies excel in their respective fields, but only a fraction eventually become revolutionary creators. The reason is that the change to a revolutionary creator, i.e., from a kid who learns rapidly in an established field to an adult who ultimately remodels a domain, is a painful transition and most prodigies want to play it safe by sticking to the conventional paths to success. What hinders child prodigies from becoming out-of-the-ordinary is achievement motivation. When achievement motivation is too high, it can crowd out ingenuity. This is because the degree to which one values achievement tends to correspond to the dread of failure. An intense desire to succeed will cause one to strive for guaranteed success rather than aim for unique achievements (Simonton, 2014).

The combination of these two factors has restrained some of history's greatest change agents and creators. Concerned with achieving normal limits and maintaining stability, they have loathed going out-of-the-ordinary. They have been persuaded, convinced or forced to take a stand rather than charge full steam ahead with confidence. They may appear to have had the traits of natural leaders, but they were figuratively, and even literally in some situations, lifted up by peers and followers. If a handful of persons had not been convinced to take an out-of-the-ordinary action, then America may never have existed, the civil rights movement could have remained a dream, and personal computers could still not be popular among other things.

Looking back today, the Declaration of Independence may seem inevitable, but the truth is that it almost failed to happen because the key revolutionaries were reluctant to take up the cause. For instance, John Adams dreaded British retaliation in the years leading up to the war and hesitated to quit his flourishing law career. His involvement came about only after his election to the First Continental Congress as a delegate. George Washington only left his farming business and joined the cause after Adams nominated him as the commander-in-chief of the army. He later wrote that he tried everything to avoid the position. Almost two centuries down the line, Martin Luther King, Jr. found himself becoming the President of the Montgomery Improvement Association and taking on heavy community responsibilities contrary to his initial goal of becoming a pastor and college president. Albeit fearful at first to lead a bus boycott, King would later overcome his trepidation and thunder his voice to unite a country around an electrifying vision of freedom. This only happened because a colleague had made a proposal to King to be the closing speaker at the 1955 Washington March and gathered a team of leaders to endorse him (Simonton, 2014).

One can only wonder how many other King's, Washington's, and Adam's never promoted, publicized or pursued their out-of-the-ordinary ideas because they were not catapulted into the spotlight. While all may not aspire to start corporations, build masterpieces, lead a civil rights campaign or change Western thought, all have ideas for enhancing workplaces, communities, and schools. Sadly, most hesitate to act on those ideas. As famously observed by economist Joseph Schumpeter (2008), going out-of-the-ordinary entails creative destruction. Promoting new systems calls for the demolition of old ones, and one should not hold back because he/she fears that the boat would rock. More than 40% of about 1000 scientists at the Food and Drug Administration admitted that they were afraid to face retaliation if they raised queries about safety concerns. In this sense, they would rather keep quiet about a critical issue that raises public awareness. Albeit America is a land of unique self-expression and individuality, the quest for excellence and fear of failure lead many to seek to fit in rather than stand out.

On Track

When people marvel at out-of-the-ordinary persons who fuel creativity and push change in the world, they tend to think that they are a different breed of humans. They imagine that out-of-the-ordinary individuals are somewhat born with an immunity to risk that causes them to be unmoved by the cost of non-conformity like the rest of society. However, the idea that being out-of-the-ordinary involves extreme risk-taking is merely a myth. Out-of-the-ordinary individuals are far more ordinary than most people realize. In all domains, those who move the world forward with out-of-the-ordinary ideas are seldom emblems of commitment and conviction. Albeit they may seem bold on the surface while challenging the status quo, inwardly they often struggle with fear, self-doubt, and ambivalence. Many think of them as the starters of their ideas, but often their efforts are fueled and even forced by others. In as much as they appear to crave risk, they really prefer avoiding it.

In a fascinating probe, researchers Jie Feng and Joseph Raffiee (2014) tracked a nationally representative cohort of over 5000 Americans between 20 and 60 years of age who became entrepreneurs from 1994 to 2008. The researchers simply wanted to find out whether persons are better off quitting or keeping their day jobs when they start a business. The survey revealed that financial need did not influence whether the founders left or held their jobs. On the contrary, the more confident risk-takers took the full plunge with spades of confidence while the more risk-averse hedged their bets by starting their corporations while still working. The study further showed that those who hedged their bets had 33% lower chances of failure than those who quit their jobs. The implication is that freewheel gambling is more fragile than risk averseness and doubting in business startup. In the case of Warby Parker, the founders hedged their bets when they launched the company. The same is true of Apple and Google founders Steve Wozniak and Larry Page and Sergey Brin.

Balancing Risk

In their day to day lives successful persons balance out risks in a portfolio. While they brace danger in one domain, they offset the overall risk level by exercising caution in another area. Such risk portfolios explain why persons often become out-of-the-ordinary in one aspect of their lives while retaining conventionality in others. A balanced risk portfolio covers one's bases financially, thus, relieving the pressure to succeed in the new venture. In this sense, "the best entrepreneurs are not risk maximizers," according to Endeavor CEO and co-founder Linda Rottenberg, rather "They take the risk out of risk-taking" (Della Cava, 2014). Managing a balanced risk portfolio means taking an extreme risk in one arena and offsetting it with extreme caution in another. Bill Gates, who is famous for dropping out of Harvard to start Microsoft waited an entire year as a sophomore before leaving school after selling a new software program. Even then, he balanced his risk portfolio by applying for an absence leave which the university formally approved rather than dropping out. In this regard, entrepreneur Rick Smith said this of him: "Far from being one of the world's greatest risk-takers, Bill Gates might more accurately be thought of as one of the world's great risk mitigators" (2009, p. 67). This was the kind of risk mitigation that led to the breakthrough of Warby Parker.

A growing body of evidence indicates that entrepreneurs, like all other persons, seem to dislike risks. Moreover, studies show that adolescents who moved on to begin productive corporations were merely taking calculated risks. Those who became successful entrepreneurs had teenage histories of parental defiance, gambling, shoplifting, etc., but were less likely to engage in hazardous exercises like drunk driving or stealing valuables regardless of the economic statuses of their parents. These finding proved that out-of-the-ordinary persons have different attitudes towards risk. While some are freewheeler gamblers, others are more cautious. To become an out-of-the-ordinary person, one must assume some risk, but the most successful out-of-the-ordinaries exercise a considerable degree of caution. Ultimately it is those who decide to champion their out-of-the-ordinary ideas who propel society. The thing that sets them apart is that they do act on their ideas.

WHAT IS "OUT-OF-THE-ORDINARY?"

A person is an "Out-of-the-Ordinary?" when that person is a combination of creativity, innovation and courage. A creative is someone that has the ability conceive something new, unusual, original or out-of-the-ordinary. An innovative person is one that acts on creative ideas. And a courageous person is one that fights through the adversity to bring change.

What is Creative

Creativity is being able to see things differently. It could be just a subtle difference or an idea that no one has ever acted on. What we need to understand is that creativity is the lifeblood of not only business, but also society. Without creativity we would reside in a static world. We are seeing less creativity coming from our children today. Many believe that standardized testing in school is thwarting growth and creativity of our children and imploring them to perfect the black and white teaching that trains them to score well on their tests.

Today, businesses are bending over backwards to promote creative thinkers. Firms are transforming their cubicle society and are now building work spaces to promote creativity. My partners at our recent firm also transformed their cubicle work space for a more creative environment. Taking a page out of the trendier firms like Google, LinkedIn, Apple, etc. they spent a fortune on the creative office. The humorous thing about this was that all the partners making this decision were University of Chicago graduates that believed in analytical, research driven decisions. Somewhere they must have done research on how to build a creative environment. They built a Tai Mahal to themselves fully equipped with a common area to promote comradery and creativity, with top of the line kitchen refrigerator including beer cooler, wine cooler and numerous comfortable overstuffed furniture and the all-important humidity-controlled guitar room. I believe that they thought if they could mimic the physical attributes of the trendy forward-thinking firms they would encourage creative thinking. Instead, the employees merely appreciated the party rooms fully stocked with booze to unwind after a long day and a great place to nap the night after. You can build an office to create, but it is not the office that creates fresh ideas. It is allowing employees time to explore and nurture ideas. Google didn't come up with Gmail because they had a cool office with nap pods, expert-in-cuisine chefs, massage programs, ball pits, lab pools, or take your pet to work days. They came up with Gmail because of their mythical policy that employees can spend 20 percent of their time on a self-directed projects.

Many firms today are bending over backwards to hire "creative" people. They are hiring splashy "internet kids" off Reddit and Instagram. Firms have spent enormous time and resources to find and hire the "Bohemians." Here is a dirty little secret…those "Bohemians" don't have any more creative ideas than my former University of Chicago "Part-nerds."

Many people believe that you are either born with creativity or not. The truth is everybody is…everybody is creative. We just need to bring that creativity out. If we want to innovate, we need to bring idea generation back. We need creativity to be innovators.

How do you generate an idea? Steve Jobs said, "innovation distinguishes between a leader and a follower." He's right. We cannot all follow if we want to succeed in this business or society. We need to lead.

So often I hear from people that they don't like their jobs, or they are unmotivated. If you think about how productive you or your colleagues are you would be amazed how little production people get done. Most professionals that track actual "engaged" work hours find that people typically work 15-20 hours of a 40-hour work week. The other time is spent chatting, eating and non-productive procrastinating. I find that mind boggling. Why is that? Why the lack of production?

The level of people's production is closely correlated with what I call "intrinsic motivation." "Intrinsic motivation" is the passion for what you are doing. The key word is passion. If you have passion for what you are doing you are always engaged.

There is much outside involvement that goes into being intrinsically motivated. If you are forced into a routine, feel that no one will listen to your ideas, or there are no avenues to make change for the positive you will be less and less productive. You, like most, will put in your 15-20 productive hours each week.

What makes you more productive is the creativity card. If you feel that you can create, present ideas, change or improve things at work you will be motivated to work harder.

Take a moment to think about your passions. What is your love? Is there something in your life that you love to do? That love, or passion might be a hobby, family or work. Whatever it is, it is what you devote a great deal of time pursuing. It is that passion, or "intrinsic motivation," that drives extreme production in that passion.

It is my experience that the most productive people in business are business owners. These people are typically passionate about their firms. That is because they are the one's making the decisions, guiding the course of the firm. Every day they are thinking what they can do to make their firm better. They are thinking creatively.

Every day they are challenging their selves. They are controlling their own destiny. They are passionate and have "intrinsic motivation."

Others that exhibit "intrinsic motivation" are those that are given the freedom and opportunity to influence the direction of the firm, department, product, etc. In business I have had small armies of people that all have similar responsibilities to accomplish a set goal. Most of my competitors had similar goals. These firms typically institute very rigid methods to accomplish the task. I have observed, and even worked at many of these firms. I know from my research and firsthand experience that they are very organized, methodical, trackable, and functional. They motivate through compensation. Compensation certainly can motivate but can also demotivate. At some point they "expect" their compensation to grow. If the compensation stagnates or declines at any point it can be very disappointing and demotivating.

Passion and "intrinsic motivation" are the driving tool that never falters. If people feel involved, important and can be heard they will be more productive. How do you "institute" passion and "intrinsic motivation" in a work force? The answer is relatively simple… encourage their abilities to make change, tap into their skills, ability, drive and creativity. A different and fresh perspective can always be advantageous. Human resources are powerful and should be encouraged. The next great idea may come from that rookie that has never spent a day in our business. Don't restrict or close ideas. Ideas are what drive great businesses. Use all resources available!

The problem we have is that we have forgotten how to be creative. We have this muscle that has gone dormant. We can get it back. If you were going to run a marathon, you would train. You wouldn't go from a couch potato to run the race without training. The same holds true for exercising your creative muscle.

Creativity, in business, is a real currency. Everybody can create, but few use it in business. We typically show up to work at the same time every day prepared to do the same thing every day, and then we leave the job at the same time every day. Our minds are trained to do that. We were not born to be drones. We were trained to be drones. We are in a rut. When we were born, we were innately creative. Over the years, our creativity has been suppressed. We need to bring that inner creativity, that is in all of us, back. It won't just re-appear. We need to train to get it back.

You must look at this like you are training for a triathlon. When you train for a triathlon you set a schedule to be ready on a specific day. You set your training schedule accordingly to be prepared on that day to compete. Your body is prepared. If you never trained for a triathlon and you were to participate in one tomorrow, the chances are you would not even show up to the race. If you did show up, chances are things would not go well. Heck, at the very least you would probably pull a few muscles.

Your brain is the same way. If we were asked to be creative today, you probably would ignore the thought and go back to what you do every day. If we did attempt to be creative, we wouldn't be at our peak creativity.

It is necessary for us to train, or jolt, our brain to be creative. Remember, creativity is a currency in the business world. The race is scheduled…let's start training.

I have created several exercises for you to train your brain to be creative again. I would suggest doing one training exercise per day to get your creativity back in shape. Later, in this book you will find a series of creativity exercises that will work those idea muscles.

According to Larry Robertson, author and researcher of many articles and books, wrote, "You might not believe it, but the best way to a big idea-an idea that changes how we think, and one that stands a mightier than normal chance of actually become real-comes from a small tweak." Roberson goes on to show us some examples to tweak.

"At the end of each work day, a nightclub manager sees food being tossed out by the ton, in his establishment and countless others across town. On his way home from work each night, he also sees dozens of homeless and undoubtedly underfed souls. For a time, the parallel observations add up minimally, until one day he "tweaks" the two separate thoughts so that they intersect one another: "What if all that wasted food could feed those hungry souls?" he wonders. 20 years on, Robert Egger's simple mental tweak has spawned programs nationwide that capture and repurpose food from restaurants, grocery stores, farms, hotels, and school cafeterias. Today, dozens of programs and organizations like DC Central Kitchen and LA Kitchen are the backbone not just of successful initiatives to feed the homeless, but of thriving catering businesses, senior citizen nutrition programs, social justice education programs, and on and on – all catalyzed by a minor mental tweak.

Now consider this example. An entrepreneur, small business advisor, and journalist spends a decade helping countless adults start and grow their own business. In the same timeframe, she and her husband are raising three kids – curious kids who wonder what exactly mom does. She knows she can't just offer them the description as she gives it to grownups. Their eyes would glaze over, and they'd never make the mistake of asking such a question again. So, she tweaks her grownup script and tells her children a story. A children's story. The fictional kind they prefer, that just happens to be about kids starting a business. The characters encounter the same challenges any adult business would, but the tale is seen, and the challenges solved through a kid's mind. The mom, host of MSNBC's Your Business JJ Ramberg, then turns the simple story into a book for kids, and the lessons of business become so simple a child can understand them. And curious children, far beyond her three, become budding entrepreneurs.

For good measure, here's one final example. A young post-doc in psychology gets a plum job on a revolutionary new research project. The goal is to figure out what really lies behind human learning, thinking, and creativity. The dominant wisdom points to intelligence as the source and the IQ test as the best indicator. But the early research results tell Howard Gardner that something's not quite right. Reality just doesn't line up with the metric. "Maybe intelligence isn't the key indicator," he first muses. But then he tweaks that thought: "Maybe it's because intelligence isn't uniform. Maybe," he ponders, "just maybe there's more than one form of intelligence." Five decades hence, no one has looked at intelligence, or creativity, or learning, the same way, and we continue to pursue the best ways in which to tap the range of our multiple intelligences." (Robertson, The Creativity Post, Aug 2017)

People often think that my mind is on the corner of creativity, leadership and innovation. I am often asked where I come up with my ideas. My answer is simple…Procrastinate. You need to get away from your day to day routine and allow your mind to produce fresh ideas. Have you ever wondered why you have some of your best ideas on vacation? It is simple. When you are on vacation you interrupt your rut. We are a society that champions processes and rituals. Our days are carbon copies of the day before and the day before, and on and on. When you are on that treadmill there is no time for fresh thinking. But, when you are on vacation, you leave the treadmill behind and now your mind has open capacity and allows you to dream and create.

For years my family has gone on a vacation to a very rural island in the Bahamas. Thirty years ago, when my wife and I first started going to the Bahamas they had no phones, TV and newspapers. Remember, this was thirty years ago which meant there was no internet, cell phones, or any of the other technology we have become accustom to. We always went on vacation during the NCAA basketball tournament. The way we got the results was by going to the beach in the afternoon, after the only flight from the states got in, we sought out the vacationers without tans to get the latest results. What we found out was that getting completely away from the treadmill allowed me to use my mind to do other things. Once we started having kids and started taking them on the Bahamas trip they became comfortable not having their technology. Now, the island has all the technology that we have in the states, but even my kids (now ages 19 to 29) still put their technology away when we are down there and find board games and create things to do. It is amazing how creative you can be if you shut everything out and allow your mind to be free to generate fresh thoughts.

That is an example of large-scale procrastination. Creativity shouldn't only come on vacations but needs to be a daily ritual. We live in a process driven word where every moment is planned. To jolt your brain from the processes of your day you need to find a slot to free the brain and let it dream. Life shouldn't be a race of perfecting your chores. In many cases you can improve on your chores by procrastinating. Psychologist, Maria Konnikova says, "Procrastination, it turns out, may not be a bad thing after all. The most effective way to tackle a new creative assignment is to put it off for a while." She continues by saying "you're actually doing the smartest and most productive thing in the world if you waste time." She is not alone in her studies on procrastination. Numerous other psychologists that have studied procrastination have found similar results. Jihae Shin did a study that shows people that played video games before work, came up with more creative thoughts than those that went straight to work. Canadian psychology professor Timothy A Pychyl also promotes procrastination by saying, "bottom line: Creative insights need time to gestate."

There are numerous examples of famous "out-of-the-ordinary" titans like Steve Jobs and Martin Luther King that were renowned procrastinators. After all it wasn't until Martin Luther King was back stage before his I have a dream speech that he came up with the line "I have a dream." It took Leonardo di Vinci sixteen years to complete the Mona Lisa. The popular online eyeglass retailer, Warby Parker, didn't finalize their website until the last minute. It is important to step back and gain perspective. Konnikova says, "to make sure to have perspective before you start working."

I'm not suggesting we all become serial procrastinator's, but rather find time in your process driven day to procrastinate and find perspective. To do that you need to jolt your system. Get off your treadmill for a moment. Change up a habit. Don't walk or drive the same way to work every day. Change up your music or reading genre. Talk to a stranger in the coffee line. Simply do something that jolts the system and you will be amazed with what a different perspective will do when tackling a mundane project. Release your mind from the everyday and let it create a new day for you and perhaps the world.

Later in the book you will find numerous creativity exercises. They are designed to jolt your brain and start thinking with more perspective.

No Creativity Without Innovation

The second leg of the three legged "out-of-the-ordinary" stool is innovation. Creativity is great. Perspective is fabulous, but without innovation that idea fizzles out. Creativity is the idea, but innovation is what makes it impactful. What is the purpose of a great idea if it has no impact. Innovation is the step where we take the creative idea and turn an invention, device, or method into something that has never existed before. Innovation is the implementation of something new.

Innovations can be incremental or radical. Every improvement that you make in products or services is an incremental innovation. Most businesses and most managers are good at incremental innovation. They see problems in the current set-up and they fix them. Radical innovations involve finding an entirely new way to do things. As such they are often risky and difficult to implement. Most larger organizations and most managers are poor at radical innovation. If you had been making LPs, then you could have introduced incremental innovations in your design and marketing. However, if this was your strategy then a radical innovation, the CD, would eventually kill you. The CD manufacturer could similarly introduce various incremental improvements. Once again, a radical innovation, music downloads over the internet, would make your offering obsolete. So, we need to constantly look for incremental innovations and radical innovations. We need to develop creativity and turn it quickly into innovation. It is the innovation of the creative idea that has impact.

I like to say the difference between creativity and innovation is how they are measured. Creativity is very subjective, so can't be measured. Innovation, on the other hand, is measurable. Innovation is about introducing change into a stable environment. Because we have a sable starting point, any innovation we bring to that environment clearly can be measured. Innovation is putting creative ideas to work. American economist, Thomas Levitt sums it up by saying "What is often lacking is not creativity in the idea-creating sense but innovation in the action producing sense, i.e. putting ideas to work."

Creativity is the fun, but riskless leg in the out-of-the-ordinary leg of the stool. It is the innovation leg that often scares away individuals and businesses. This is where one must start spending time and money on ideas. As an innovator you wrestle with two issues: risk-taking and failure aversion. As I mentioned in an earlier chapter, a great idea does not mean great results. Even great ideas can be a flop. Dean Kamen's Segway idea passed all the "this is going to change the world" tests but proved to be a flop. Even though the Segway fails, Dean Kamen did not pursue other great ideas. Yes, you want to attack an idea with both eyes open and realize that even with all the proper research a great idea does not guarantee great results. All innovation involves inherent risks, but a failed idea should never be a black mark, but rather as knowledge and education that you can apply to your business with future ideas. Andrew C. Marshall, an Innovation Consultant, summed up by saying, "Creativity is important in today's business world, but it's really only the beginning. Organizations need to foster creativity. Driving business results by running ideas through an innovation process puts those ideas to work – for companies and their customers. Creativity is the price of admission, but it's innovation that pays the bills."

Got the Guts

The last step to be "out-of-the-ordinary" is having the courage to act on creativity and innovation. Courage takes on many forms. Courage comes in physical, moral, social, and creative courage.

In Rollo May's book <u>The Courage to Create</u> May says, "Society is in the midst of change. Change causes many to experience a sense of alienation and purposelessness. We have two choices: either to withdraw and panic, or to develop the courage to create a better society. The second choice requires courage, and of course, creativity.

Courage means to move ahead even when moving ahead seems hopeless. This courage must be centered in our own being; it is the courage of our convictions and underlies all other virtues and values. Without courage we could not exist or transform our society or ourselves. There are four types of courage.

1. Physical courage that does not deal with muscles or violence, but with the body as a way of cultivating empathy and sympathy.
2. Moral courage that takes a stand against violence of any type: physical, moral, spiritual, and psychological. The most frequently experienced form of cowardice is the statement, "I did not want to become involved."
3. Social courage which includes risking oneself to achieve meaningful intimacy, to invest one's time, emotions, energy over time in order to develop relationships. It is the courage to withstand the fear of autonomy, abandonment and self-actualization. It is also the courage to stand up to the fear of being totally absorbed by the other.
4. Creative courage, which includes both the discovery and the appreciation of new forms, ideas, patterns and symbols. It is the courage to defy death, not by denying physical death, but by reaching beyond it through the products of our creative acts. Creativity comes from the struggle and

courage to confront death and to rebel against it. Courage means seeing death as an injustice and fighting it and all injustice."

If you are like most, and follow others, this analogy hopefully helps you find the courage to become a leader and not a follower. I often tell a story of a herd of zebra grazing in an open field. This story has a great deal of synergies with our society today. One of the main reasons our society is mostly followers is because of the theory that there is strength in numbers. Being a follower will seldom make you a difference maker in business or society. So why are we serial followers. The answer is safety. If we do as the others do and we fail, then we all fail. Followers don't want to fail alone, but if we all fail then we feel better that we are in similar company. The problem with this theory is that you are limiting yourself from being a success. There is something inherently wrong about that logic, but it appears to be a very logical theory in practice today. We, as a society, are followers of the theory "strength in numbers." One of the best ways I can debug this theory is to tell the herd of zebra grazing in an open field story. If you visualize a herd of zebras in a vast field, they are typically together in a herd. Why is this?

Protection! Right? We assume they huddled together for protection. Apparently, the herd also believes in the theory of "strength in numbers." Now think about it. They stand there and say, *"If we stay together we will be better protected from the predators."* Does this strategy work? If the predator attacks, are they all protected? The ones in the middle certainly are protected, right? At the end of the story, let me know if the zebra in the middle are safest. Let's get back to the story of the zebra grazing. While grazing, the herd moves around as a group. They move in multiple directions to eat fresh grass. If you are the zebra positioned near the middle of the herd, are you getting the fresh grass? No. The zebra on the outside of the pack are eating the fresh grass. In the simple theory of "strength in numbers," the safest zebras in the middle eat the trampled down, already grazed grass. The zebras on the outside, which appear to be the most vulnerable, are eating the freshest, non-trampled grass. Here is where the theory starts to fall apart. The zebras on the outside are getting more nourishment, which should make them bigger, stronger, and faster.

So, when the predators decide they are hungry, they attack the herd. In all the chaos, what happens to the herd? They scatter. Every zebra for themselves. What happened to the first layer of protection, the zebras on the outside? They are gone. They are thinking survival. They are fleeing the danger as fast as they can.

Who gets caught? The ones who thought they were the safest because they were in the middle of the pack. But the reason they weren't the safest is because they didn't get the fresh grass. They were less nourished and became the weaker animals. That equates to being slower and less nourished than the zebras on the outside of the herd. The predators aren't stupid. They're not going to chase down the faster zebras. They are there to eat, not to exercise. They attack the slowest ones. They don't want to overwork for their meal.

So, if in society we continue to live inside this herd of safety, we could become prey to the predators. I will argue that the safest place to be is not inside the "strength in numbers" circle, but on the outside where you have the courage to be on the outside of the protection, with the ability to get bigger, faster and stronger. To flourish in society and business, we need to break away from the pack. We need to be the people on the outside eating the fresh grass.

How do we become the ones outside the pack, the ones eating the fresh grass? We need two things. We need to generate the courage to foster your creativity and innovation. You need the physical courage to be prepared for the hard work, the moral courage that what you are doing is right for society, the social courage to face all the detractors and nay-sayers, and the creative courage to seek out new ideas and thoughts through creative reflection,

To be a leader in today's business, and society, you can't just be creative, innovative, or have courage, you need all three. To be "out-of-the-ordinary" you will need all three characteristics.

ROSES CAN BE TORNY

The dawning of the 21ˢᵗ century saw the invention of the Segway take Silicon Valley by storm. The Segway was widely hailed by tech industry kingpins like Steve Jobs and Jeff Bezos, with John Doerr, the famous investor who had betted successfully on Google and several other blue-chip startups, pumping $80 million into the business and predicting it would be the fastest corporation ever to reach $1 billion. Doerr also predicted that the Segway would surpass the Internet in significance as it was set to transform cities and lives. Nevertheless, Segway never became profitable, and today it is only sold in niche markets (PandoDaily, 2013). In contrast, when the pilot for the TV series *Seinfeld* debuted, it was dismissed as a dismal failure. The outcome was the same a year later when the series went live. Just when one of the writers was ready to give up and walk away, the network ordered half a season to replace a canceled show. Consequently, the show remained at the top of the Nelson rating over the next decade and brought in more than $1 billion in earnings, even becoming the top TV series in the United States (Mellor, 2014).

When society bemoans the absence of ingenuity/out-of-the-ordinary thinking, the blame often falls on the lack of creativity. Nevertheless, the greatest hindrance to out-of-the-ordinary thinking is not the generation of ideas, but idea selection. Society does not necessarily suffer from a shortage of novel ideas. On the contrary, it is constrained by the lack of persons who are experts at identifying the correct novel ideas. The Segway turned out to be a great miss. Seinfeld, which was a false negative and widely expected to fail, ultimately thrived.

No Guarantees

Segway's inventor, Dean Kamen, was described as the modern Thomas Edison. He already had a track record of remarkable breakthroughs: he was the brainchild behind the portable dialysis machine and the portable drug infusion pump among a host of other inventions which had earned him the National Medal of Technology and Innovation, the highest honor for invention in the United States. The Segway was Kamen's most unique invention and, in fact, he himself predicted that it would eventually replace vehicles the same way that cars replaced horses. But can inventors be objective when assessing their own ideas?

In one study, researcher Justin Berg (2016) showed different groups of people recordings of circus performances and then requested them to project how well each would perform. The first group of persons were circus artists, and these mostly gave positive predictions about their own videos, anticipating to excel. Circus managers, likewise, submitted their projections. In testing the accuracy of the forecasts, Berg measured the actual success of each performance by tracking how the members of the general audience (over 13,000 persons) liked, funded, and shared the videos. It turned out that the circus artists were terrible at forecasting how the audience would judge their performances. On average, they ranked their videos two slots too high against nine other circus artists. The managers were more realistic in their rankings as they were considerably distanced from the performances, which placed them in a more neutral position (Berg, 2016).

It is a proven fact that personal evaluations are often fraught with overconfidence. In the creative field, this bias can especially be hard to overcome. All new ideas are unique, and while earlier inventions may have sold out well, the new one is still different. Further, when one develops an idea, one is often too close to personal tastes and too distant from the audience to make a correct evaluation of the idea. Overconfidence can indeed help inventors and entrepreneurs to some degree as it motivates them to pursue their goals. However, it can also cause them to fall victim to confirmation bias, which is when they focus on the strong points of their ideas while discrediting their limitations after learning the preferences of their audience.

In music, Beethoven was deemed a perceptive self-critic, yet his own favorite symphonies, which included quartets and sonatas, are not the ones that posterity has often performed and recorded. Psychologist Aaron Kozbelt (2007) analyzed letters in which Beethoven had rated 70 of his compositions and compared the appraisals with expert judgment. Kozbelt found that Beethoven had made fifteen false positives. Eight pieces turned out to be minor albeit he had anticipated they would be major pieces, and eight false negatives, which were pieces that turned out to be major even though he had initially criticized them. In all, Beethoven had a 33% error rate notwithstanding that most of his assessments were made after getting feedback from the audience.

If creators knew that they were fashioning a masterpiece, they would only halt their efforts to generate ideas when they struck gold. However, they often backtrack, going back to iterations that earlier on they had cast aside as inadequate. In Beethoven's Fifth Symphony, which is his most celebrated work, he scrapped the conclusion of the first movement as it felt quite short and only came back to it later. Had he been able to tell the extraordinary from the ordinary, he would have embraced his composition then as a hit.

The question, therefore, that begs is if out-of-the-ordinaries cannot judge the quality of their ideas reliably, how then do they maximize their chances of making a masterpiece? The answer is that they simply generate a large number of ideas. Psychologist Dean Simonton (2011) found that creative geniuses were not qualitatively better than their peers in their fields. They merely produced more work which afforded them a greater variation and raised their odds of being out-of-the-ordinary. This led Simonton to the conclusion that the odds of coming up with a successful or influential idea is a positive function of the total number of generated ideas.

Considering Shakespeare, for instance, many are familiar with only a few of his classics, not remembering that he also produced 154 sonnets and 37 plays within two decades. In fact, in the same five-year span that he produced three of five of his most cherished works, i.e., *Macbeth, Othello*, and *King Lear*, he also released *All's Well That Ends Well* and *Timon of Athens*, both of which though relatively average, have consistently ranked among the worst of his plays and have been bashed for incomplete plot and character development and unpolished prose. Being out-of-the-ordinary indeed involves much work. Simonton (2011) moreover observed that persons also produce their most out-of-the-ordinary works when they produce their largest volumes of work. In the case of Edison, for example, he pioneered the phonograph, the carbon telephone, and the light bulb between the ages of 30 and 35 during which time he also filed over 100 patents for other diverse inventions including stencil pens and a technique for preserving fruits.

The assertion that a tradeoff must always exist between quantity and quality such that one does less work to produce better works is a fallacy. In fact, as far as idea generation is concerned, quantity is the most predictable path to ingenuity. Most persons fail to become out-of-the-ordinary because they only fabricate a few ideas and then obsess about perfecting them. While working on the Segway, Kamen was conscious of the blind variations that characterize the creative process. With more than 440 patents to his name, he had numerous misses and hits. He encouraged his engineers to explore many variations to raise the odds of stumbling into the right one. However, he settled on the Segway before considering all ideas for resolving transportation issues, forgetting that inventors always have to struggle hard to rate their product accurately.

The best way to improve one's judgment of ideas is by gathering feedback. In the case of the Segway, however, Kamen did just the opposite. He maintained a high degree of secrecy, fearing the idea would be stolen or the basic concept would go public too soon. Only an elite group of investors were allowed to try it out during development. Albeit the development team came up with a wide range of ideas, critical input from customers which could have helped make the right decisions for the final product was lacking. The device underwent more than three iterations before any customer saw it. The lesson is that conviction in one's own ideas can be lethal because one is left vulnerable to false positives, as well as hindered from generating the requisite variety to achieve one's creative potential.

Looks Can be Deceiving

Managers would often prefer to avoid risks and focus on the cost of investing in wrong ideas as opposed to the benefits of piloting good ones. When the very first Seinfeld script was handed in, executives did not know what to make of it and quickly rated it as weak. In fact, such false negatives are not a rare occurrence in the entertainment industry. Looking back into the past, one can see that studio executives had passed on hits such as *Pulp Fiction, Star Wars,* and *ET*. In publishing, not a few managers rejected *Harry Potter, Lord of the Flies, The Chronicles of Narnia, Gone with the Wind,* and *The Diary of Anne Frank*, but by 2015, J. K. Rowling's volumes alone had sold more copies than any other book series and generated more than $25 billion. The records of corporate inventions are littered with stories of managers who ordered their employees to cease work on projects that later became big hits, from HP's electrostatic displays to Nichia's LED lighting. Microsoft nearly buried the Xbox and Xerox almost canceled the laser printer as impractical and too expensive.

When faced with uncertainty, the first instinct of most persons is usually to avoid novelty, scouting for reasons why unfamiliar ideas might fail. Managers tend to vet novel concepts with an evaluative mindset. In a bid to hedge self against the risks of poor bets, they contrast new notions with templates of ideas that thrived in the past. Publishing executives sidelined *Harry Potter* because they thought it was too long for a children's book. In the case of the *Seinfeld*, Brandon Tartikoff felt that it was "too New York and too Jewish to appeal to a broader audience. Professor Erik Dane (2010) of Rice University notes that the more experience and expertise that persons gain, the more they become entrenched in a given way of viewing the world. He cites studies of bridge players in which the experts struggled more than the novices to adapt when the rules were modified. Another study found that novice accountants were better off than experts at applying a new tax law. The implication here is that persons become prisoners of their prototypes as they gain more knowledge about a domain.

Although in theory audiences should be more receptive of novel concepts than managers because they lack the blinders that go along with expertise and have little to lose in any case, in practice, they are no better than managers at forecasting the success of new ideas. Focus audience groups are bound to repeat the mistakes of the managers because the audience evaluates a program against an established set of ideas of how it should work instead of engaging with it. In the case of *Seinfeld*, test audiences found many flaws in it, e.g., lacking *ALF's* relatability, the family aspects of *The Cosby Show*, and the community of *Cheers*. Thus, both test audiences and managers are unfit judges of creative ideas. They are too inclined to false negatives. Creators likewise struggle with being too confident of their own ideas. However, the one group of forecasters that are close to gaining mastery are fellow creators assessing each other's ideas. While studying circus acts, Berg (2016) noted that peer circus artists were the most accurate predictors of the likeability of videos of fellow artists. They were roughly twice more accurate than the audiences and managers in predicting whether a video would be shared.

The implication here is that persons should turn more often to colleagues rather than seek feedback from managers or assess own out-of-the-ordinary ideas. Colleagues have no stake in the ideas of peers, thus, are unaffected by the risk aversion of test audiences and managers. This guards against false negatives and allows them to identify unusual possibilities in their colleagues. Having no stake in the ideas of colleagues allows peers to give honest appraisals.

When evaluating new concepts, the best way to avoid false negatives is by thinking like creators. In a set of experiments, Berg (2016) asked a group of adults numbering over 1000 to predict the success of novel products in the marketplace. He presented several useful ideas, conventional ideas, as well as ideas that were less practical to raise the odds of persons correctly ranking useful ideas first rather than favoring conventional ideas. Half of the participants were assigned to think like managers by spending 6 minutes developing a list of three criterias for analyzing the success of new products. The group then made correct bets on useful novel ideas 51% of the times. However, the other group was more accurate and chose the most promising new concepts 77% of the times. The difference came about because the second group engaged in a creative rather than a managerial mindset just for six minutes. This experiment proved that developing out-of-the-ordinary ideas improves one's ability to pinpoint the potential in an unusual thing. Further, to raise the odds of betting on the most out-of-the-ordinary ideas, one must generate own ideas just before screening the suggestions of others.

Well Rounded Titans

A recent study that compared all scientists who won the Nobel Prize from 1901 to 2005 with typical scientists of their eras found that albeit both groups attained deep expertise in their study fields, the winners of the Nobel Prize were dramatically more likely to participate in arts than their less accomplished counterparts. The study was repeated with thousands of Americans, and the results were the same for inventors and entrepreneurs: those who began businesses and contributed to patent applications had a higher likelihood of having leisure time hobbies involving drawing, architecture, sculpture, literature, and painting than their peers. These results show that interests in the arts among eminent scientists, entrepreneurs, and investors reflect their aptitude and curiosity. However, it is not that certain kinds of out-of-the-ordinary persons seek out exposure to the arts, but the arts also serve as powerful sources of creative insight (Root-Bernstein et al., 2008).

Just as investors, entrepreneurs, and scientists discover novel ideas by broadening their knowledge to include arts, so likewise can society members gain breadth by increasing cultural repertoires. A recent study by strategy professor Frederic Godart found that creativity in the fashion industry is highly influenced by the time spent working abroad. Fashion directors who manifested the greatest creativity were those who had spent the longest time working abroad and in more diverse cultures. Further, the greater the difference between the foreign and the native cultures, the more creativity the directors manifested (Godart, Maddux, Shipilov, & Galinsky, 2015). This model lines up with the Rick Ludwin's experience with *Seinfeld*. Ludwin, the manager who aired the first half season of *Seinfeld*, had a broad background in TV equivalents in several very different nations, which allowed him to see promise where others saw only doubts.

Know Thy Customer

A study led Erik Dane found that a person's intuitions are only accurate in those fields where one has much experience. For instance, if one confronts a patient's symptoms as a physician or enters a burning house as a firefighter, the experience will make one's intuitions more accurate. However, for political forecasters or stockbrokers, the past has no reliable implications for the present.

The reason is that the world is rapidly changing, and the environment is increasingly becoming unpredictable. The result is that intuition is now less reliable as a source of insight on new ideas and persons need to engage in more analysis. Studies further show that the odds of one performing poorly in a new field are directly proportional to the successes that one has had in the past. This is the hubris that treads along with success, and it stems from the fact that past successes can cause one to become overconfident and fail to seek critical feedback when seeking to invest in a wholly new field (Dane, Rockmann, & Pratt, 2012).

When Dean Kamen pitched the Segway, he was very passionate about it. He predicted that urban centers would become too clogged with cars and the Segway would be the solution. Steve Jobs, who was renowned for making big bets based on intuition as opposed to systematic analysis, was seduced by the novelty of the concept and predicted it would be a straight hit. Jobs, however, got it wrong this time because of three primary reasons: the Segway was out of his domain of software and hardware, enthusiasm, and hubris. On the other hand, when the Warby Parker entrepreneurs first came up with their idea of selling eyeglasses online, they first sought extensive feedback from potential customers and fellow manufacturers. The result was that they had a great deal of success. Had Kamen followed this process with the Segway, a lot more critical feedback could have rolled in to prevent its development or lead to its redesigning into a more useful product. Nevertheless, although the Segway may have failed, Kamen is still a promising inventor. Whether evaluating or generating new ideas, the future is unpredictable, and the sooner this truth is internalized, the better.

Pitfalls of Creative Thinking

Being "out-of-the-ordinary" can come with pitfalls. While most businesses and business leaders are asking for creative and innovative ideas, most don't really mean it. The problem is that people are threatened by change, work, and competition.

This behavior runs wild through our society. We are often taught to keep our head down and our mouth shut. Just saying that sounds ludacris, but that is standard operating procedure for most. This thinking has been ingrained in our society from a very young age. In grade school we were taught to listen quietly and speak when spoken to. If we were to question the teacher on materials, methods, or practicality we would be deemed a troublemaker.

Once we got into the work force things appear to be changing. The people of authority are now telling us to think outside-the-box. However, they may be saying that, but they really don't mean it. A typical manager doesn't want anyone rocking their status quo. After all a good idea could threaten their status quo. Not only do managers not want to change their status quo, but they definitely don't want to listen to someone who works under them.

Most businesses and organizations are built around structure and processes. An "out-of-the-ordinary" idea could threaten those processes and structure. After all, they could make those processes and structures obsolete. That may be good for the company as whole but would threaten those whose roles are to run the current structures and processes. Once people are threatened by what would happen if there was change, the chances of those ideas ever being implemented are slim to none.

In those rare cases when you find a manager that will entertain your idea, there becomes that fear that the idea fails, which means they fail. Again, another obstacle to improving the greater whole. Then there is the case of bandwidth. Most employees believe that they have reached their bandwidth compacity. Even if they recognize that an idea can improve the organization they don't want to work any harder than they are currently are.

Many businesses and organizations are linear. They have spent tremendous time and resources in putting everything in particular boxes. Every box has a pecking order and purpose. When an idea can shake a box, the initial reaction is to protect the turf and fight change. If you are a "out-of-the-ordinary" person that is often sharing your ideas you can be considered, by many, as pushy or difficult. Does anyone really want to be considered a problem person? Eventually you will be pushed out or you will fall in line with the status quo.

I have witnessed and experienced all these pitfalls. When you see some of the most successful business leaders in the world, they typically started their own business. There is a reason why. These people believed in themselves and choose to control their own destiny. These people are our entrepreneurs. Highly successful "out-of-the-ordinary" people that run businesses typically respect and encourage "out-of-the-ordinary" thinking and frown on middle management road blocks. So, if you are in a linear business model you will need to maneuver around the road blocks gracefully, but there is also a good chance that they are not a good match for you.

HIGH WIRE ACT

In the 1990s, Carmen Medina, then a high-flying CIA analyst, went to Western Europe on a three-year mission. Upon return, she found that she had backtracked in her career, and consequently got stuck from one job to the next that neither fitted her skills nor aspirations. This led her to probe other ways to contribute to the intelligence community and started attending working groups that concern the future of intelligence. During her time in the CIA, Medina noted a critical communication problem in the intelligence community. The default information-sharing strategy was via "finished reports," which were released once each day and was hard to relay across the agencies. Analysts could not share insights as they arose. With national security on the line and lives at stake, each second mattered. Medina perceived a need for a radically different system that would permit real-time updates sharing among the agencies. Her proposal was widely countercultural: that intelligence agencies commence publishing their reports and findings instantaneously, transmitting them over the classified intelligence community Internet, i.e., Intelink (Kelly & Medina, 2014).

This suggestion was quickly shot down for her colleagues strongly believed that the Internet was insecure, and thus a threat to national security. All would be jeopardized if knowledge were to land in the wrong hands. Nevertheless, Medina did not back down. Having seen the efficiency of the fax machine brought into information sharing, she was persuaded that the digital revolution would transform the intelligence world and did not relinquish her quest. Finally, she became fed up with the disrespect she was receiving and got involved in a shouting match that resulted in her taking a three-day sick leave and commence a new job hunt. She failed to find a new job and was demoted in the agency. Consequently, she kept her peace for a while. Three years later, however, she again began to champion the online system for real-time reporting across agencies. Less than a decade later, Medina played a fundamental role in the creation of the Intellipedia, intelligence agencies' internal Wikipedia for accessing each other's knowledge. This was radically at odds with the norms of the CIA that an observer commented that "it was like being asked to promote vegetarianism in Texas" (Grant, 2017, p. 65).

Intellipedia became a critical resource to intelligence agencies, and by 2008 it was widely used in tackling diverse challenges such as identifying the masterminds behind the Mumbai attacks and securing the Beijing Olympics. The site accrued over a million pages and more than 500,000 users within the intelligence community within a few years so that it won the Service to America Homeland Security Medal. So, the question that begs is how come Medina failed in her initial efforts and what caused her to gain an audience the second time? It is a fact that the world changed between these two periods. The Internet got a broader acceptance, and the 9/11 attacks sounded an alarm bell for better coordination between the intelligence agencies. Also, Medina herself rose to be the deputy head of intelligence at the CIA, and so she gained the power she needed to push for the Intellipedia (Kelly & Medina, 2014).

The Boat Can be Rocked

Managers and leaders often appreciate when employees take up the initiative to offer help, construct networks, accumulate new knowledge, and ask for feedback. However, many do not appreciate their suggestions on leadership and often penalize such boldness.

One study across service, retail, nonprofit, and manufacturing settings found that the more often employees voiced their notions and issues upward, the less likely they were to earn promotions and raises. In another experiment, individuals who failed to speak out against racism criticized those who did as self-righteous. This gives the idea that the top of the moral ladder can be a rather lonely place (Fragale, Overbeck, & Neale, 2011).

To understand the hurdles Medina had to overcome, one needs to separate the two key dimensions of social hierarchy which are often bundled together, i.e., status and power. Power entails exercising authority or control over others. Status, on the other hand, is when one has the admiration and respect of others. Alison Fragale, a professor at the University of North Carolina, conducted an experiment in which persons were punished for attempting to exercise power with no status. When disrespected persons tried to exert an influence, others saw them as hard, self-serving, and coercive. It appears the others were saying such persons had no right to tell them anything for they had not earned their admiration (Fragale et al., 2011). This was what had happened to Medina; she had lost status while she was abroad. She had no opportunity to prove her worth to her colleagues, and so they gave her no credence. Frustration mounted as people brushed her concerns aside.

Often, when one finds that persons are disrespectful, one becomes resentful, and in a bid to assert authority, one resorts to increasingly disrespectful conduct. This vicious cycle was most shockingly demonstrated when researchers asked participants to work in pairs on tasks, with one participant given the power over what the other would do to have a chance to earn a $50 bonus. Power holders were randomly assigned, and they mostly chose reasonable assignments when they learned that their peers respected and admired them. They would have their peers write about their experiences the previous day or tell a funny joke for the $50 bonus. However, when they learned their peers disdained them, they retaliated by setting up tasks that were humiliating, such as bark like a dog three times or say "I am filthy" five times. Merely being told that they were disrespected almost doubled their odds of using power in ways that disrespected others.

Medina's circumstance did not reach this far, but as she continued to speak up, trying to exercise power without status, she was increasingly resented. Status must be earned or granted but not claimed. Years later in her second attempt, Medina did not jeopardize her career by trying to attack the system from below rather she sought status by becoming a part of the system and then changed it from within. This strategy was perfectly in tune with the observation of Francis Ford Coppola, the iconic filmmaker that "The way to come to power is not always to merely challenge the Establishment, but first making a place in it and the challenge and double-cross the Establishment." The second time Medina made the risky choice of presenting her notions again, she made her risk portfolio more stable by taking up a job that focused on information security. Thus, even though her case for sharing information over the Internet had earlier on seemed like a security threat, now she could frame it as a part of her goal to enhance security.

So, as she gained the respect of her colleagues, she accumulated idiosyncrasy credits, which alludes to the freedom to deviate from group expectations. Idiosyncrasy credits are earned through respect rather than rank. After taking up the job in security, Medina spent the subsequent months making significant advancements in the digital domain. She did work that furthered the mission of the agency and consequently earned sufficient idiosyncrasy credits to push her vision for knowledge sharing. She received a promotion to the executive level and in 2005, two agency analysts, Don Burke and Sean Dennehy, united to help develop the Intellipedia. Medina afforded the senior-level support that was essential to catapult the concept into the real-time application (Kelly & Medina, 2014).

Starting With Plan Z

After having their first child, Alisa Volkman and Rufus Griscom were horrified by the numerous false advertisements and wrong counsel offered about parenting. This led them to start their own blog network and online magazine, which they called Babble, to challenge the prevailing parenting clichés and confront the bitter truth with humor. When Griscom presented Babble to venture capitalists in 2009, he issued a slide containing the top five reasons to not invest in his business, precisely the opposite of what an entrepreneur should do. Rather than killing his business, this strategy worked, and that year Babble earned $3.3 million in funding. Two years later when Griscom went to Disney to pitch it for sale, he employed the same strategy listed the reasons why anyone should not buy the website. Contrary to expectation, Disney did end up acquiring the company for $40 million (Kafka, 2015).

Many people tend to think that one must stress strengths and downplay weaknesses to be persuasive. This strategy can indeed work well if the audience is supportive. However, audiences tend to be skeptical when one is pitching a novel concept or suggesting a change. Investors seek to poke holes into one's reasoning, and managers tend to hunt for reasons to believe that one's ideas will fail. Under such circumstances, Griscom's technique is the best way forward as firstly it disarms the audience. The focus of the audience is shifted to trying to resolve the problem rather than seeking to defend self against undue influence. Medina had failed to acknowledge the shortcomings of her ideas when she first spoke up about them. A friend even confided to her that she spoke as though she might never be happy unless opposition to her ideas ceased. In her second effort, however, she demonstrated more balance in her presentations, even expressing doubts about her own ideas.

Leading with the limitations of an idea also helps one to look smart. Griscom points out that reviewers always feel an obligation to list some shortfalls about a product. This way they think they were not snowed, but rather that they are discerning. Thus, by leading with the problems at Babble, Griscom showed investors that he was not misled by his own ideas and neither was he trying to mislead them. On the contrary, he was smart enough to do his own research and expect some issues that they would identify. Thirdly, leading with the downside of one's ideas boosts one's credibility. When Griscom made known the challenges he faced with Babble, he came out as not just knowledgeable but also modest and honest. It is true that highlighting shortcomings can backfire when an audience had no knowledge of them in the first place. In Griscom's case, however, the audiences were already skeptical. Moreover, they were set to find many more problems with due diligence. Thus, informing them of the shortcomings of the business model did not just do them service but also established trust. In addition, the approach leaves audiences with a more favorable evaluation of the idea due to the bias in which individuals process information (Kafka, 2015).

You Don't Know it All

After spending a considerable amount of time working on an idea, the rhythm and melody of the idea gets imprinted onto the creator's heart. At this point, it is barely possible to imagine how it sounds to a listening audience for the first time. The result is that one can end up under-communicating own ideas. The critical challenge of presenting an out-of-the-ordinary idea is to make an audience hear the accompanying tune that the creator of the idea can hear in his/her own head. When John Kotter, a Harvard professor, examined change agents in the mid-1990s, he noticed that they tended to under-communicate their visions by a factor of ten, i.e., they spoke ten times less about the direction of change than stakeholders needed to hear. The outcome was that employees did not understand the vision, let alone internalize it (Kotter, 1996). The point is that if one desires his/her out-of-the-ordinary concept to be understood, then one must speak it up and repeat it over and over until the idea sinks in. Familiarity breeds comfort rather than contempt.

The reason is that exposure increases the ease of processing. Unfamiliar ideas, on the other hand, need more effort to be understood. It is critical to note that over-familiarity can cause boredom. In speaking, however, audiences seldom reach their saturation points. Evidence suggests that liking tends to rise as persons are exposed to a concept between ten and twenty times and more complex ideas may still need additional exposure. Moreover, exposures have been noted to be more effective when they are short and blended with other ideas that help sustain an audience's curiosity. Medina employed the same concept of familiarity when she introduced the idea of open information sharing in the CIA as the deputy head of the agency. She began a blog on the classified intranet to model the transparency she was pushing for and wrote short commentaries twice every week giving her views about the need to reduce secrecy and share news as the future wave. Albeit at first several heads reflexively brushed the concept aside, the short presentations interwoven with other communication caused the leaders to warm up over time. Soon the agency's technology experts built a platform using the intranet that made it possible for individual employees to set up own blogs. Ultimately, the intelligence community got an active blogging scene where analysts across agencies share information informally.

When to Bail

Economist Albert Hirschman (1970) outlined four options for handling a dissatisfying situation: exit, voice, persistence, and neglect. To exit is to remove one's self from a displeasing situation. Voice entails actively trying to better the situation. Persistence entails trying to bear with a situation, whereas neglect involves staying in the same situation but reducing one's effort just enough to keep things running. These choices are essentially based on feelings of commitment and control. Employees who feel they are stuck with the status quo will be neglectful if they are not committed to the organization and persistent if they have some degree of commitment. Those who feel they can make a difference but still are uncommitted will exit. On the other hand, those who care deeply and believe their actions do matter will speak up.

Medina was partly shuttered when her initial attempts to voice her ideas were silenced. She confessed that what kept her in the agency was her immediate boss, Mike, whom she described as being "prone to cynicism and mercurial." She described Mike as a disagreeable manager with a skeptical stance toward others (Kelly & Medina, 2014). Disagreeable managers are more disposed to challenge the status quo and improve the ability of their subordinates to speak up effectively. Studies show that such managers tend to embrace new concepts more often and feel less threatened by the contributions of others. They are more concern with improving the organization as opposed to defending the status quo. They do not turn a blind eye to the organizations shortcomings.

As Medina rose up the ladder in the CIA, she noticed that colleagues grew more receptive of her suggestions while middle managers brushed them off. The reaction from the middle managers can be explained by the middle-status conformity effect–the effect of the middle segment in the hierarchy of organizations being dominated by insecurity, leading members to passively follow the leader so as to avoid being singled out. Thus, Medina opted to voice her ideas downwards and upwards as opposed to horizontally. She gained credibility among the senior leaders, as well as junior employees, and rising stars in the agency became excited about her vision and accorded her status. Medina also pointed out that the fact that she was female in a male-dominated agency and that she had a double minority status made it especially difficult for her idea to gain acceptance initially. In fact, she believed she only got it through by quietly advancing the agenda and only began voicing her sentiments after gaining enough support (Kelly & Medina, 2014).

Don't be a Yes Person

Another case involves Donna Dubinsky who was the distribution and sales manager of Apple in 1985 when the CEO Steven Jobs suddenly proposed to do away with all six warehouses in the United States, dropping their inventory, and advancing to a just-in-time system of production in which computers would be assembled on order, and the FedEx would overnight them. Dubinsky saw this concept as a grand error that could jeopardize the company's future. She initially held her peace, believing that the proposal would simply fade away, but when it persisted, she voiced her concerns. She was, however, overruled. Eventually, she got assigned to a task-force that investigated Jobs proposal for several months. In the final meeting, Jobs asked if all agreed with his proposal. Most agreed. Dubinsky ended up with a 30-day ultimatum to come up with a counterproposal or leave Apple. She came up with a new proposal of strengthening customer service centers, which was adopted in place of the just-in-time production. Dubinsky later confessed that she was heard because she was known to do her job well and deliver. Albeit opposing Jobs may have seemed like a losing battle, Dubinsky knew she was advocating for the company rather than herself (Jick & Gentile, 1995).

Contrasting Dubinsky's and Medina's experiences raises important questions about how best to handle dissatisfaction. Neglect is not an option when searching for out-of-the-ordinary ideas. Persistence is but a temporary route to earn the right to speak up, but ultimately it maintains the status quo and like neglect fails to resolve one's dissatisfaction. Thus, the only viable options for changing a situation are voice and exit. In the case of exit, Dubinsky later left Apple in 1991 because she was frustrated that the corporation did spin off Claris as a separate company. Claris was one of Apple's subsidiaries and in which Dubinsky had held a senior position in international sales and marketing. She joined Palm Computing as a startup and under her leadership, the company developed the PalmPilot, which became the first runaway success in the still young market for personal digital gadgets. She did move to other companies due to one dissatisfactions and still had great breakthroughs. She, later, confessed that she was among those who kept Jobs from creating a phone and her departure from Apple was what helped catapult the iPhone into existence.

The decisions of Medina and Dubinsky have crucial lessons for aspiring innovators. While one chose to voice, the other opted out; but the central point is that they never stayed silent. Ultimately, the errors one will always regret are those of omission and not commission. Medina and Dubinsky were left with few regrets when they chose to express, rather than censor, themselves.

PULLING IN THE REINS

In work and in life, society often teaches that acting early and promptly is the key to success. This belief is even preserved in a proverb, i.e., "the early bird catches the worm," implying that hesitations leads to losses. Speed indeed has its clear advantages: one can be sure to finish what he/she began and beat rivals. However, for out-of-the-ordinary individuals, the disadvantages of prompt action often tend to outweigh the benefits of the same and by far. Knowing just when to take an out-of-the-ordinary action is critical and procrastination can be as much a virtue as it is a vice. Hesitation may be risky, but the delay can also save one from placing all eggs in one basket. Being out-of-the-ordinary does not necessarily mean that one must be first: the truth is that the most successful out-of-the-ordinaries have always been out of schedule.

Day Dreaming

Although procrastination may impede productivity, it nonetheless can be a resource for creativity. Jihae Shin, a creative doctoral student, gathered data from a Korean furniture corporation and noted that those employees who often procrastinated and spent more time in divergent thinking were seen by their supervisors as significantly more creative. Procrastination itself did not fuel creativity: stalling only set them back if they lacked the intrinsic motivation to resolve a major problem. However, when they were passionate about forging novel concepts, procrastination resulted in more creative solutions (Shin, 2015).

Ancient civilizations had early learned the benefits of procrastination. In ancient Egypt, two different verbs were used to describe procrastination; one denoted laziness while the other one implied waiting for the opportune moment. In this sense, it may not be a coincidence for some of history's most out-of-the-ordinary thinkers like Leonardo da Vinci to have been procrastinators. Da Vinci's out-of-the-ordinary achievements spanned sculpting and painting, music and architecture, engineering and mathematics, cartography and geology, and botany and anatomy. Scholars postulate that he took a considerable time to paint the *Mona Lisa*, commencing in 1503 and going on and off for not a few years before finally completing it just prior to his death in 1519. While critics thought he was wasting his time toying around with optical experiments and like distractions which kept him from finishing his paintings, it turned out that these distractions were critical to his being out-of-the-ordinary (Pannapacker, 2009).

Da Vinci took almost fifteen years to develop the ideas for *The Last Supper* while working on various other projects. Twelve years later, it was the basis of the new horizontal arrangement of thirteen seated at a dinner table in the famous painting. Da Vinci perceived that being out-of-the-ordinary could not be rushed. He realized that geniuses at times do the most when they work the least, for they are contemplating inventions and forging the correct ideas in their minds (Pannapacker, 2009).

I Have a Dream

Early in the summer before his famous "I Have a Dream" speech, King sought counsel from three close advisers regarding the right tone and content. Then King had a lengthy talk about the address with his lawyer and speechwriter, Clarence Jones. Later,

King requested Jones and one other activist to begin working on a draft. Over the following weeks, King suppressed the urge to foreclose on a direction or theme. He waited till only four days before the march to actively start working on the address. On the last night, he assembled a group of advisers to return to the drawing board. Jones (2011) recalls that King wanted the ideas reviewed one last time to have the best approaches.

By delaying to flesh out and firm up the speech, King allowed Jones to profit from the Zeigarnick effect–the effect of having a better memory for incomplete than complete tasks. Jones had held a meeting with Governor Nelson Rockefeller, a noted philanthropist who supported civil rights, four months earlier when he sought funds to bail King out of the Birmingham jail. Rockefeller handed Jones a briefcase with $100,000 and banking rules mandated that he sign a promissory note, which again Rockefeller paid for. On the night before King's speech, Jones reminisced about the experience with Rockefeller and decided that the promissory note would be a powerful metaphor. Consequently, King used it in his speech on the following day. This event revealed one benefit of procrastination, which is that it allows one to accumulate the broadest set of ideas at one's disposal (Jones, 2011).

Wing It

From the moment that King gave his momentous speech until now, four words remain etched onto the collective memory of society: "I have a dream." This phrase remains one of the most cognizable phases in history. Surprisingly, the "dream" idea was never a part of the speech. While King was addressing the crowd, Mahalia Jackson, his favorite singer, shouted from behind, "Tell 'em about the dream, Martin!" (Jones, 2009, p. 56). This was what launched King into his inspiring vision of the future.

Besides allowing time to develop novel concepts, procrastination also keeps one open to improvisation. Advanced planning normally closes the door to creative possibilities that may spring from one's field of vision. Berkeley psychologist Donald MacKinnon (1962) found that America's most creative architects tended to be more spontaneous than their technically skilled but ordinary peers, who thought themselves as more conscientious and self-controlled. Strategy researchers Pol Herrmann and Sucheta Nadkarni (2010) studied about 200 corporations in India and noted that the most profitable ones were those whose CEOs gave the lowest ratings of self on promptness and efficiency. In both scenarios, it is those executives who admit to wasting time before settling down to work and who at times fail to pace themselves and get things done on schedule that are the most successful. Such habits can stall progress on tasks, but they also open up leaders to be more strategically flexible as in the case above. When CEOs are too meticulous with plans, subordinates tend to perceive them as rigid. The more flexible and versatile a CEO is, the more appealing he is before subordinates.

Politician Drew Hansen (2005) writes in "the Dream" that by the time King was done with his speech, he had added so many new elements to what he had initially prepared that the length of his address almost doubled. Several of the lines relating to the dream had been improvised, but King had already rehearsed their variations in earlier speeches. He had a wealth of material, including Bible verses, own sermons, lines from favorite poets, etc., at his disposal and could draw upon these extemporaneously to authenticate his delivery. King demonstrated that while great out-of-the-ordinaries are great procrastinators, they nevertheless do not skip planning.

Timing Matters

Idealab founder Bill Gross had been involved in the startup of more than 100 companies. Afterwards, he ran an analysis to establish what drove failure versus success and found the most crucial factor to be timing. In his own words, "Timing accounted for 42% of the difference between failure and success" (Team YS & Khera, 2017). American society firmly believes in a first-mover advantage, i.e., Americans disdain followership and esteem leadership. Marketing researchers Gerard Tellis and Peter Golder (1993) conducted a classic study in which they compared the successes of corporations that were either settlers or pioneers. The pioneers were mostly first movers, i.e., the first company to create or sell a product. The settlers, on the other hand, took their time before launching and only entered markets after pioneers had made them. Golder and Tellis (1993) analyzed hundreds of brands in 36 different product lines and were struck by the staggering difference in failure rates: 8% of settlers against 47% of pioneers. Settlers were about six times less likely to fail than pioneers. Moreover, pioneers only captured 10% of the market when they survived as opposed to settlers who captured 28%. It turned out that the shortcomings of being a first mover were bigger than the merits.

Marketing researcher Lisa Bolton (2006) points out that even when persons learn that evidence does not support the first mover advantage, they still cherish it. According to Bolton, the myth of the first-mover advantage can be shattered best by asking persons to give reasons for first-mover disadvantage. When out-of-the-ordinary individuals make haste to become pioneers, they are bound to overstep, and this overstepping is the first setback of first movers. One study of over 3000 startups found that three of every four fail due to premature scaling, i.e., making an investment that the market cannot support. Secondly, there is sufficient justification to believe that first-movers are usually risk-seekers and are prone to make impulsive decisions. The more cautious entrepreneurs, on the other hand, wait in the sidelines and watch for the right moment and then balance their risk portfolio before entering a market. Strategy researchers Barnett and Pontikes (2014) found that entrepreneurs had higher odds of success when they waited for the market to cool down than when they rushed to join the crowd into hyped markets.

Thirdly, settlers can improve on rivals' technology to better their products. Pioneers make all the mistakes themselves all the while settlers watching and learning from those errors. The fourth disadvantage of first movers is that pioneers often get stuck in their initial offerings. Settlers, on the other hand, can perceive the market changes and the changing consumer tastes and make appropriate adjustments. They have the pleasure of waiting for the market to ripen up. A review of the US automobile industry over a century revealed that pioneers had lower odds of survival as they grappled to establish legitimacy. They also came up with routines that did not suit the market and got outdated when customer needs changed. On a different note, the founders of the Warby Parker had to wait for Zappos, Blue Nile, and Amazon to get persons comfortable with buying items online, which they would typically not order online.

The notion of waiting for the right time applies beyond the business world. In Medina's case, for instance, the CIA was not ready for the idea of digital information sharing back in the early 1990s. It was only after electronic communication became more familiar and secure that the agency became receptive of her idea. It should be noted, however, that being first is not always unwise. Someone must always be a pioneer. Pioneering is mainly disadvantageous in underdeveloped, unknown, and uncertain markets. The key point is that it is a mistake to rush an out-of-the-ordinary concept to beat competitors.

Youth vs. Experience

Economist David Galenson (2011) explains that although society is quick to remember young geniuses in the sciences and arts, there are also many old masters who soar much later. In film, for instance, for every Orson Welles, who made the first feature film, *Citizen Kane*, at 25; there is an Alfred Hitchcock, whose masterpieces—*Vertigo, North by Northwest*, and *Psycho*—were made late in his career when he was 59, 60, and 61 respectively. The time one reaches the peak of ingenuity and how long this peak will last depends on one's thinking style. In his study of creators, Galenson identified two types of innovators: conceptual and experimental. While conceptual creators fabricate grand concepts and launch out to execute them, experimental innovators resolve issues via trial and error method and learn as they advance.

Galenson (2011) saw conceptual innovators as sprinters and experimental innovators as marathoners. In his review of Nobel Prize-winning economists, he noted that conceptual innovators made their most cherished accomplishments at the age of 43 while experimental innovators made theirs at 61. In poetry, conceptual innovators composed their best pieces at 28 while experimental innovators did theirs at 39. Among Nobel Prize-winning physicists, half of the young geniuses below 30 were conceptual innovators whereas 92% of the masters who were above 45 did experimental work. The basic differences between experimental and conceptual innovators explain why some out-of-the-ordinary persons bloom late while others peak early. Galenson also found that conceptual breakthroughs often happen early because the innovators approach a problem with a fresh mind, which makes it easier for them to assemble a striking out-of-the-ordinary insight. However, they become less innovative once they get entrenched in conventional ways of doing things. This had been Einstein's problem after he had developed the theory of relativity. After he had internalized the fundamentals of relativity, he struggled to get to terms with deviation from those tenets as demanded by quantum physics.

Conversely, experimental innovation is a more sustainable source of out-of-the-ordinary ideas as it entails working over the years to amass the necessary skills and knowledge. For instance, it took Roger Sperry years of experiments with human patients and split-brain cats to figure out the working of the two brain hemispheres. In this sense, adopting an experimental approach to gather expertise and sustain out-of-the-ordinary thinking as aging creeps in is the best bet for all persons. This approach served Da Vinci well, not to mention King, who gave his "dream" speech in his 20th year of public speaking about civil rights. Sprinting may indeed be an excellent strategy to a young genius, but it takes the patience of experimentation to run a marathon.

CAT FIGHT

Albeit she is largely forgotten today, Lucy Stone did more for women's suffrage in the United States than any other person. When she took her stand for women's rights in 1855, she moved thousands to follow in her footsteps and brand themselves Lucy Stoners to pay her homage. Her league over the next century included poet Edna St. Vincent Millay, artist Georgia O'Keeffe, and aviator Amelia Earhart. Some of the women today who qualify as Lucy Stoners include Sheryl Sandberg and Sara Blakely. Stone was the first woman in America to keep her own name after marriage, which was just one of her numerous firsts. She was the first female Massachusetts resident to earn a bachelor's degree. She became the first American full-time lecturer and advocate for the rights of women. She also became one in only a few women who ever spoke in public, leading national conventions and taking part in the launch of the *Woman's Journal* that ran for almost half a century and to which the suffrage movement owes its success (Kerr, 1992).

Stone's remark at the 1851 women's rights convention is what is widely believed to have sparked the flame in the women's rights movement. Calling upon women to petition for property and voting rights, she announced, "We want to be something more than the appendages of society" (Kerr, 1992, p. 60). Her words flew across the Atlantic to inspire British philosophers Harriet Taylor Mill and John Stuart Mill to publish an essay on women enfranchisement that became quite popular and helped mobilize the English suffrage activists. In America, Stone's speech inspired Rochester teacher Susan B. Anthony to join the suffrage movement, and the two along with Elizabeth Cady Stanton, the other great suffragist of the time, collaborated as the renowned heads of the suffrage crusade. Long before they could attain their shared goal of equal voting rights, however, their league crumbled.

Stanton and Anthony ceased collaborating with Stone in 1869 and went on to create their own women's suffrage organization. A feud ensued between the former allies, and they fought bitterly as rivals. They published own newspapers, petitioned funds separately, and lobbied legislatures independently. The hatred that Stanton and Anthony cherished toward Stone was very intense insomuch that they decided to write her organization out of their history of the suffrage campaign. This division caused the suffrage movement to lose not a little credibility in the public eye and nearly led to its demise (Kerr, 1992). The key question in this event is what led to such a heated and destructive conflict among three leaders who shared a profound commitment to the same cause? Through an analysis of the challenges that these three women faced and other examples, it would become evident that constructing effective coalitions entails striking a delicate balance between pragmatic policies and venerable virtues. Goldilocks concept of coalition formation is a key insight to this end. Forming alliances between opposing factions calls for the tempering of the cause, cooling it to the lowest possible temperature. However, drawing allies into the cause requires a moderate tempering to just the right temperature.

Less Alike

Albeit it is widely assumed that common goals cement groups, the reality is that they split groups. Dartmouth psychologist Judith White identified the idea of horizontal hostility as one lens for understanding the fractures. Even though they share key objectives, radical groups tend to regard the more mainstream groups as sellouts and imposters, and White saw horizontal hostility everywhere. A deaf woman wins the Miss America crown, and rather than cheering her on, deaf activists protest that she was not deaf enough because she spoke orally. In another case, a Black Students Association objects the appointment of a light-skinned black law professor at one university because she was not black enough. To explain why such animosity occurred, they did a fascinating study on horizontal hostility in different minority groups and movements (White & Langer, 1999).

In one study, vegans demonstrated almost thrice as much hostility towards vegetarians than the vegetarians towards the vegans, with the vegans citing that mainstream vegetarians were simply wannabes and cared much less about the cause. In another study, orthodox Jews judged conservative Jewish women more negatively than liberal Jewish women. The message was apparent: true believers are wholly in. The more firmly one identifies with an extreme group, the more one will seek to differentiate self from the more moderate factions that threaten the values of the cause (White & Langer, 1999). It was such horizontal hostility that led to the schism between Lucy Stone and Anthony and Stanton. Stone was more moderate/mainstream whereas Stanton and Anthony were relatively radical. The earth began to crack when Stanton and Anthony partnered with George Francis Train, who was a known racist. Train supported the suffrage movement as he thought women could help reduce the influence of African Americans. This outraged Stone (Kerr, 1992).

The rift between the three women widened when Stanton and Anthony stood against the proposal of the Fifteenth Amendment to give African American men voting rights. Stanton and Anthony made this decision so as to reach liberal constituents who were for the amendment. Stone, who was more sympathetic to the abolitionist cause, tried to bridge the black activists and her two colleagues. Stanton and Anthony, however, interpreted Stone's efforts as treason against the women's cause. They consequently backtracked on their commitment to a joint organization and formed their own suffrage organization the following week. Stone's efforts to reconciliation bore no fruits, and the two organizations maintained their separation for over two decades, even working at cross purposes in some cases (Kerr, 1992).

The split adversely affected both sides of the suffrage movement, and they needed new allies. They got one who was highly unlikely: The Woman Christian Temperance Union (WCTU)–a women's organization that was formed to combat alcohol abuse, for drunken men often propagated domestic violence and caused poverty in their families. Unlike the suffrage groups, the WCTU was very conservative, with members comprising upper- and middle-class women with strong traditional values and religious beliefs. Notwithstanding the differences between the WCTU and the suffrage groups, coalitions between the two organizations formed in nearly all states (Kerr, 1992). The puzzle is why did WCTU agree to support suffragists?

Northwestern University sociologists Brayden King and Wooseok Jung and Stanford University's Sarah Soule tracked the rise of unusual alliances between social movements like gay rights activists, the peace movement, etc., and found that shared tactics were a crucial predictor of alliances. Groups found affinity when they employed similar engagement methods despite their causes (Jung, King, & Soule, 2014).

Lucy Stone recognized that common goals could not suffice for the prosperity of a coalition and noted that "persons will differ as to what they deem the best means and methods." Likewise, Stanton acknowledged that the methods were the critical issue between the two suffrage movements. Stone was committed to state-level campaigns, involved men in her organization, and sought to inspire change via speaking and meetings. Stanton and Anthony, on the other hand, desired a federal Constitutional amendment, favored an exclusively female organization and were more confrontational. The more moderate activists consequently forged alliances with temperate activists in the WCTU and together they persuaded many states to allow women to vote. Thus, the suffragists learned a great principle about winning allies (Kerr, 1992).

Unplug Me

In 2011, Meredith Perry, then a college senior, perceived a serious flaw with technology. Technically everything that used to be wired was now wireless, yet she still needed to plug in her phone and computer to charge them. Consequently, she began thinking of things which could beam energy into the air and settled on ultrasound. When she made her proposal known to her physics professors, they bushed it off and claimed it was impossible. She got the same response from ultrasonic engineers and even some of the world's top scientists. Perry nonetheless won an invention competition, and consequently was challenged to demonstrate the technology. As a single beginner of a technology startup, she needed allies to proceed, and the challenge was extreme. In her own words, "Every single person who is now working for the corporation either did not think it was viable or was extremely skeptical." She reached out to many technical experts who were quick to pinpoint flaws in her physics and mathematics that they would not even consider working with her (Hitt, 2013).

Finally, Perry decided that rather than explaining the working of her concept, she would merely give the specifications of what she wanted. This approach worked. She convinced two acoustic experts to fashion a transmitter, and a third to model a receiver. An electrical engineer dealt with the electronics. Soon enough she had collaborators on board, including professors from Stanford and Oxford, with math simulations that confirmed the viability of her theory. This was enough to draw the first round of funding, which came from a chief technology officer who initially had been highly skeptical (Hitt, 2013). While communicating the purpose behind ideas is good for inspiring the masses, it may not work when doing something out-of-the-ordinary that challenges the status quo.

Researchers Meyerson and Scully (1995) found that out-of-the-ordinary individuals must always become tempered radicals to succeed. The reason is that the values they believe in often go against the grain, and so they must learn to tone down their radicalism by forwarding their ideas and beliefs in ways that are more appealing and less shocking to mainstream audiences. Perry was one such tempered radical. She made an implausible concept plausible by concealing its most extreme features. Thus, she managed to persuade technical experts who could not take a leap with her, to agree to take a few steps. This outcome demonstrates that out-of-the-ordinary persons can tone their radicalism down by smuggling their true aspiration inside a Trojan horse.

In the case of coalitions, when members refuse to temper their radicalism, they often fall apart. In the women' suffrage movement, Stone and heT husband warned Anthony that enlisting Train's support would cause irreparable damage to the cause. Anthony, however, stuck to her radical conviction that if women could not get voting rights, then neither should blacks. She maintained her campaign with Train all through Kansas, and when Stone faced her about soiling the reputation of their movement by associating it with Train, Anthony became defensive and accused Stone of envy and hatred of her paper. Stanton supported Anthony. The alliance with Train, however, proved costly. The suffrage movement lost the vote in Kansas, which ironically had been the very first state to adopt the cause. Anthony and Stanton did not learn their lesson and refused to tone down their extreme stance that all who supported suffrage were allies (Kerr, 1992).

After forming their own organization, Stanton and Anthony teamed up with Victoria Woodhull, an activist who formerly had been a charlatan healer and a prostitute, and who advocated for sexual freedom. This alliance triggered a severe storm of criticism from all quarters, and members pulled out of Stanton's organization in great numbers insomuch that they could not hold a convention. Stanton had failed to see the benefit of tempered radicalism in her alliance with Woodhull. Thus, she drove both past and potential allies away. Albeit the suffragists saw Anthony and Stanton as the group's representatives, outsiders perceived Woodhull negatively because she held the most extreme views, and her scandal overshadowed the cause, leading to the alienation of many who were open to the more moderate idea of voting rights, but were closed to the radical notion of sexual independence for women (Kerr, 1992).

Who to Trust

Studies show that relationships tend to be positive, negative or ambivalent. Ambivalent persons/frenemies are those who may offer their support at one time and undermine one at another time. Stone's relationships with Anthony and Stanton were deeply ambivalent. While she admired Anthony's industriousness and Stanton's wit, she objected to their "wild alliances" and "lunatic friends" that threatened the credibility of the movement. Anthony and Stanton even signed Stone's name to an ad commending their racist benefactor without her approval. In 1872, which was after the split in the suffrage movement, Stanton reached out to Stone for reconciliation. Stone took some conciliatory steps but declined an invitation to Rochester NY to settle their primary differences once and for all (Kerr, 1992).

From a superficial point of view, Stone's decision may seem stubborn, but research shows that dealing with inconsistent friends can be quite exacting emotionally. In fact, research indicates that ambivalent relationships are unhealthier than negative ones, with higher rates of dissatisfaction, depression, and stress. Stone knew the risks of forging alliances with ambivalent ties. Since she could not control or predict the behaviors of either Anthony or Stanton, she opted to keep her organization free of them. Albeit the first instinct for many is to break bad relationships and save ambivalent ones, evidence suggests that the reverse is in fact what one should do.

Feeling Comfortable

The movie *Lion King*, like many other out-of-the-ordinary ideas, never really got off the ground initially. It was conceptualized as "*Bambi* in Africa with lions" (rather than deer as protagonists). After the initial failure, five of the writers came together to rethink the script. They contemplated weaving an idea about the succession of Kings and finally pitched the story to a group of executives at Disney. It took quite some debating before finally Maureen Donley proposed the idea of *Hamlet,* in which the uncle kills the father, prompting the son to seek revenge. In that critical moment, the movie got the green light. What happened when Maureen Donley suggested *Hamlet* as the script is that the executives' familiarity with *Hamlet* helped them connect the novel script to a classic narrative, which gave them one point of reference. Being entirely out-of-the-ordinary can indeed cause one to lose an audience; hence, the need for familiarity and fondness (Grant, 2017).

In the suffrage movement, suffragists presented two key arguments to earn the right to vote: societal reform and justice. The justice argument focused on equality between women and men, which was deemed radical. The temperate movement was conservative and did not want anything to do with such a cause. The societal reform argument, on the other hand, was more moderate and focused on social good and stressed women's moral qualities. The justice argument did not prevail with the WTCU members, and the pitch had to be reframed to gain wider acceptance. The new WTCU leader Frances Willard rephrased the suffrage cause as "Home protection ballot." Safeguarding the home was a familiar vision for the members of WTCU, and they could now use suffrage to a desirable end (Kerr, 1992). While radical thinking may be necessary to plant an out-of-the-ordinary concept on the ground, tempered moderation is needed to sell it to a broader audience. Willard would never have begun the suffrage movement, but her credibility with the temperate activists allowed her to rally their support to the cause. She, like Perry, smuggled the vote for the suffrage cause inside the Trojan horse of "home protection."

Let's Get Along

Stanton and Anthony ultimately saw the benefits of tempered radicalism. They avoided radical leagues for more than a decade and invested their energy in educating the masses. Anthony and Stone even saw eye-to-eye and ultimately joined forces to become one team. This, however, did not come before a splinter group of radicals broke away from Anthony and Stanton's organization for not wishing to league up with the "temperates," so to speak. Stone's last words were "Make the world better" (Kerr, 1992, p. 187). She died in 1893 and was hailed by friend and foe alike. It would be 27 more years before the passage of the Nineteenth Amendment that allowed women full rights to vote. Stone's imprint of tempered radicalism was nevertheless powerful and visible in its passage (Kerr, 1992).

ROCKING THE FOUNDATION

To become out-of-the-ordinary, one must be willing to embrace some risk. The reason is that one can never be sure of success. Jackie Robinson braved hate mails, racist peers who would not play with or against him, and opponents who cut him with their spiked cleats deliberately from the time he became the first black player in the Major Leagues Baseball. He went ahead to become the first black vice president of a key American corporation and the first black baseball announcer in the United States (Falkner, 1995). The question, therefore, that begs is what gave him the nerve to rise against social norms and remain resolute in the face of physical, social, and emotional risks? Some clues can be found in the family backgrounds of baseball players who have shared his habit of stealing bases.

Psychologist Richard Zweigenhaft and science historian Frank Sulloway identified more than 400 brothers who played professional baseball and contrasted persons from same families who shared half their DNA and had a similar upbringing to investigate why some baseball players did steal more bases than others. The result revealed that birth order predicted the sibling who would attempt to steal more bases, i.e., the likelihood of younger siblings to try and steal a base was 10.6 times higher than their older brothers. It is not that the younger players had better skills than their elder brother, but rather they had a greater propensity to take risks. Besides trying more steals, younger siblings had 4.7 times greater odds of being hit by a pitch as they dared to crowd the plate more often. Moreover, younger brothers had 3.2 greater chances of stealing a base safely than their older brothers and their appetite for risk increases their likelihood of taking part in riskier sports such as rugby, boxing, ski jumping and the likes (Sulloway & Zweigenhaft, 2010). Jackie Robinson himself had been the youngest among five siblings. Firstborns opted for safer sports like golf, cycling, tennis, and baseball among others. This difference also features in science and politics, with grim ramifications for intellectual and social progress.

Sulloway's (2010) analysis of reactions to the theory of evolution among scientists from 1700 to 1859 proved that later-borns may be more prone to rebellion than firstborns. Before Darwin, 56 of 117 later-born scientists believed in evolution in contrast with only 9 of 103 firstborns. 16 years after Darwin published his findings, the odds of later-borns dropped from 9.7 times to 4.6 times greater than firstborns. Firstborns now became more confident in advocating for evolution than before because the ideas had gained a wider scientific acceptance. It is critical to note that the age of the scientists did not affect the difference between the later-borns and the firstborns.

Trouble Maker

Stanford professor James March (1994) explains that most persons follow a logic of consequence when they make decisions, i.e., which course will yield the best outcome. While pursuing this course, one always finds reasons not to take risks. However, when one follows the logic of appropriateness, one thinks less about that which will guarantee the results of one's wishes and instead acts more on the visceral sense of what one ought to do. Pundits have for years touted the advantages of the firstborn. As the eldest child, he/she is typically set for success, profiting from the undivided time, energy, and attention of fawning parents.

A recent study by economists Giorgio Brunello and Marco

Bertoni on the impact of the order of birth on career success found that when entering labor markets, firstborns enjoy 14% higher starting incomes than later-borns. Moreover, firstborns' profit from greater education that allows them to command the higher wages. However, the researchers noted that this career advantage vanishes by age 30. The reason is that firstborns are more averse to risks than later-borns. Laterborns, on the other hand, tend to have poorer starts, i.e., low achievements in school, bad smoking and drinking habits, etc., probably because they find these initial preoccupations distasteful. However, because they are more adventurous than firstborns, they tend to shift to better-paying occupations sooner and more often, allowing them a faster salary growth (Bertoni & Brunello, 2013).

Birth order does not determine one's personality but only affects the probability that a person will develop in a certain way. Rebels are twice more likely to be later born than firstborns. While firstborns tend to be dominant, ambitious, and conscientious, later-borns tend to take more risks and embrace out-of-the-ordinary ideas. Thus, while the former tend to defend the status quo, the latter tend to challenge it. Two reasons why later-borns tend to take risks are sibling rivalry and the mode of parental upbringing (Bertoni & Brunello, 2013).

Niche Picking

The one common aspect among siblings is that they have big personality differences. Niche-picking might help explain this phenomenon. Physician and psychotherapist Alfred Adler contended that since firstborns commence life only as children, they first identify with their parents. However, when younger siblings arrive, firstborns face a risk of being "dethroned," which leads them to emulate their parents by enforcing rules and asserting themselves over the younger sibling, thus, setting the stage for rebellion. Faced with physical and intellectual challenges of directly competing with an older sibling, younger siblings opt for a different way to stand out. The eldest child takes the niche for the responsible achiever, and it is difficult for followers to usurp him/her. Niche-picking explains in part why siblings are often very different (Bertoni & Brunello, 2013).

Jackie Robinson participated in track-racing in college but could not beat Mack, his elder brother, who was five years his senior. Mack won a silver medal in the Olympics 200m dash. Robinson differentiated himself by lettering at UCLA in baseball, football, basketball, and along with track and field, where he won a NCAA broad jump championship (Falkner, 1995).

Relax in Time

Parents tend to commence as strict disciplinarians with firstborns and then their flexibility increases as the number of children increases. Further, when siblings serve as role models and surrogate parents, one will face fewer rules and punishments besides enjoying the security of their protection. One also tends to begin engaging in risks earlier. With five kids to feed, Mallie Robinson, Robinson's mother, needed to work, so she delegated the task of feeding Robinson to her eldest daughter, Willa Mae. Willa fed, bathed, and dressed Robinson and even took him along to school while Frank, Robinson's elder brother, always defended him in fights. Consequently, Robinson joined a gang when he grew older and was caught shoplifting and stealing frequently. Mallie often failed to enforce punishment on him but instead complained to the police captain that he was being harsh on Robinson (Falkner, 1995). Herein is a clear shift in parenting standards.

While the risk-taking tendencies of many out-of-the-ordinary persons can be explained by their unique autonomy and protection that they got as babies in their families, such parenting habits also can nurture rebellion among children in any rank in the birth order.

Sulloway (1997) points out that predicting personality is more difficult with only children than with those who have siblings. The reason is that they tend to have the experience of both firstborns, i.e., growing up in a world of adults, and lastborns, i.e., receive fierce protection. Thus, the evidence on the order of birth stresses the necessity of allowing children the freedom to be out-of-the-ordinary. One danger of this course, however, is that the child might misuse the privilege (of freedom) and become rebellious and put self and others at risk. So, the question that begs is what determines which direction one will channel his/her out-of-the-ordinary thinking?

Lots in Common

Samuel and Pearl Oliner carried out a pioneering study on non-Jews who put their lives on the line to rescue Jews during the Holocaust and compared them to a group of neighbors who never extended a helping hand to the Jews. The two groups; bystanders and rescuers, had a lot in common, including similar occupations, neighborhoods, religious and political beliefs, and educational backgrounds. They were also equally rebellious in their childhoods, i.e., individuals in the two groups stole, lied, and failed to follow instructions. However, what differentiated the rescuers was how their parents addressed misconduct and rewarded good conduct. The rescuers pointed out that their parents primarily used a rational approach to discipline, which involved explaining why something was wrong and focusing on moral values. Research has also found that this is the same approach that characterizes the parents of adolescents who refrain from deviance and parents of out-of-the-ordinary individuals who challenge the status quo in their fields (Oliner & Oliner, 1992).

How parents explain rules to their children matters a lot. Recent studies have found that teenagers break rules when they are forcefully enforced over them. On the contrary, when parents give a clear rationale for rules, the odds of breaking them decline significantly as teens internalize them. Reasoning, however, also tends to create more rebelliousness in as much as it leads to rule following. The reason is that by expounding on moral principles, parents foster voluntary compliance with rational values in their children but also encourage them to question rules that contradict important values. The Oliners further discovered that while the parents of the bystanders focused on compliance with rules for own benefit, the parents of rescuers encouraged their children to contemplate how their actions would affect others. The result was that the rescuers could empathize with the sufferings of the Jews (Oliner & Oliner, 1992).

Robinson used to practice all kinds of mischief: hurling rocks at cars, pilfering food from local stores, stealing golf balls. He was at one point taken to jail at gunpoint. However, a mechanic, Carl Anderson, observed the behavior of the gang and took him aside and warned him that his conduct would hurt his mother. Robinson confessed that he was too ashamed to tell Anderson how right he was. That piece of advice marked a turning point in his life (Falkner, 1995). It should nevertheless be noted that values are formed not just by the way parents react when their children misstep but also by the way they react when they do good things.

Parenting 101

Children can have a great deal of freedom if parents will explain to them the consequences of their actions to others and stress how moral choices exemplify good character. This will improve the odds of their expressing out-of-the-ordinary impulses in the form of creative or moral actions. However, while parents can nurture the desire to be out-of-the-ordinary, persons must find their own role models at some point in their own fields. For Robinson, Carl Anderson was just one such role model, as well as Branch Rickey, the owner of the Dodgers who recruited him to step over the color barrier. Albeit finding the right model may not be easy, one can always look through history for such.

REASON FOR THE DECLINE IN CREATIVITY

Creativity is a unique and valuable trait that plays an important role in our everyday life. According to psychologists, creativity is the ability to produce original and adaptive ideas (Linkner). Behavior, ideas or products that are both valuable and novel must occur to prove the existence of creativity. Ideas presented must be new and functional to allow an individual to adjust according to situations at hand, or be able to solve problems that arise unexpectedly. It has been vital in bringing and maintaining human civilization worldwide. Creativity can be grouped into two; historical creativity and psychological creativity. Picciuto and Carruthers state that true creativity is when the novelty is associated with a whole society or ancient tradition while psychological creativity is when the novelty is relative to one individual (Picciuto). Psychological creativity is more prominent than historical and to some extent, a trait possessed by almost every human being, although in varying degrees. In the 18th century, Roman mythology indicated that every human being was born with a "guardian spirit" which always determined the individual's fate and individuality. Later, the role of the "guardian spirit" was shifted and people started to believe it was responsible for determination of a person's special talents or aptitudes. Although it was initially perceived that everyone possessed the unique mental capacity, it was later discovered that mental capacity varied and the term genius suited those identified to have mental capability above average (Picciuto).

Furthermore, outstanding creativity was a gift from spirits or gods and not an individual's act. However, according to new philosophies of science, human beings can contribute or boast the creative ability through training. As Spanish philosopher, Ortega y Gasset stated, "it is necessary to insist upon this extraordinary but undeniable fact: experimental sciences have progressed thanks in great part to the work of men astoundingly mediocre, and even less than mediocre. That is to say, modern science, the root, and symbol of our actual civilization, finds a place for the intellectually commonplace man allows him to work therein with success" (Simonton). It is through this that there was the emergence of academies of art to train students on creativity. For instance, artist-teacher Sir Joshua Reynolds of the British Royal Academy of Art; he used to advise his students on ceasing to depend on their genius but instead allow the industry to improve talents one possessed (Simonton). Previous researches conducted by various notable psychologists provide an explanation of the development and rise of creativity over centuries. Moreover, many of the existing researches on creativity address substantive issues which are directly related to creativity such as insight, problem-solving, talent, intelligence and genius (Simonton).

However, in recent years, the topic of creativity has been of concern, with the main issue being declining creativity. In the United States, the shift in educational, economic and political views since the 1990s have significantly affected the outbox thinking of students in the country. In the years before the 1990s, American education was known to cultivate, encourage and inspire students. Schools were known to provide students with an opportunity and freedom to think alone, critically and differently. However, with the introduction of test-centric education, creativity has declined.

The Evolutionally Approaches to Psychological Creativity

Human creativity is indeed unique and has continued to bring transformations across the planet. By analysis of archaeological artifacts, it is evident that human creativity began about six million years ago when ancestral humans started to diverge from the ancestral apes. The adoption of a larger brain might have caused the ancestral human to engage in self-triggered recall and rehearsal in light of dynamics and structures involving associative memory. The functionality of neurons was improved which in turn evoked the forging of creative connections. In the second increase in the human brain which took place between 600,000 and 150,000 years ago, the explosion of creativity in the Middle/Upper Paleolithic took place and this time set the germ of modern-day representation of thoughts and cognitive processes (Gabora). Besides, the Upper Paleolithic is considered in some instances as the "big bang" of human culture since it exhibited more innovations compared to those that were realized in the prior six million years of human evolution. Evolution of the modern humans commenced around 250,000-300,000 years ago and was characterized with human brain enlargement as a result of biologically evolved cognitive advantage.

According to the Diffusion of Innovation (DOI) Theory, ideas or products acquire momentum and spread across a given population or social system. The process allows individuals, who are part of that social system, to adopt ideas or behaviors to perceive things in an improved manner. According to researchers, adopters occur in five distinct categories namely innovators, early adopters, early majority, late majority, and laggards (Orr). Innovators are those individuals who aspire to try an idea first and are always eager to take a risk. Early adopters are mostly leaders who like change and are always ready to adopt an innovation. On the other hand, the early majority refers to individuals who are not leaders, but they adopt new ideas before the common people. The late majority refers to people who are always skeptical of changing. These people only adopt change after it has been tried by the majority. Lastly, the laggards are individuals who are bound to traditions and therefore very conservative. These people are bound by tradition and very conservative. Most countries which are currently experiencing declining creativity can be termed to have a majority of their citizens falling in the last three categories.

From a Darwinian Theory perspective, the evolution of creativity is in most cases influenced by culture and the process of natural selection. As Darwin put it, is there a way of an organism to withstand biological change after accumulating traits over a lifetime? Darwin's aim was to explore how living things can adapt over time despite getting new modifications now and then. He realized that although acquired traits can be discarded, those inherited are more likely to exhibit in coming generations (Gabora). The theory explains individual and population level of change regarding the distribution of variants. In our analysis of declining creativity, Darwinian Theory can be used to explain the rise and fall of creativity scores over the years. Practices and things keep on changing worldwide and therefore the shaping of our thoughts and behavior by distinct evolutionary forces. Therefore, having a foundation knowledge and understanding of the evolutionary origin of human creativity places us in a better position to understanding current pressing issues concerning creativity. Besides, it provides us with an insight into how we can utilize our creativity to forge the future of human species as well as our planet.

The Emergence of the Creativity Crisis

In 1958, Ted Schwarzrock was only 8-years old and a third grader when he joined the "Torrance kids," a group which consisted of 400 Minneapolis kids who had finished a series of creativity tests designed and administered by professor E. Paul Torrance (Bronson). As Schwarzrock states, he could still recall, vividly, the occasion when a psychologist gave him a fire truck and asked him,

"How could you improve this toy to make it better and more fun to play with?" (Bronson). The response he provided excited the psychologist to the extent he was able to rattle off 25 improvements in the psychologist's notes. Such an impressive response and many others made scholars describe him as an individual who had an "unusual visual perspective" and "an ability to synthesize diverse elements into meaningful products" (Bronson). Torrance Tests of Creative Thinking (TTCT)-Figural was a standard assessment of creativity and those who recorded perfect results in the creativity index turned out to be successful adults in the future. Those who thought and presented ridiculous ideas on Torrance's tasks grew up to be inventors, doctors, entrepreneurs, college presidents, software developers, authors, and diplomats. Kyung Hee Kim, at the College of William & Mary, performed analysis on almost 300,000 Torrance scores of kids and adults and discovered that creativity scores rose steadily since the discovery of the assessment tool until 1990 (St John). After that, the scores started to fall consistently, and according to Kim's observations, it was clear creativity among American children, from kindergarten to the sixth grade, was diminishing. A reverse creativity score continues to be recorded, an indication of declining creativity in the United States.

In the mid-1980s, America shifted into an age of insecurity, and this resulted in the implementation of various changes in the educational, economic, political, social and technological sectors. The era marked the birth of American's decrease in creativity. Insecurity in the nation manifested in various forms among them domestic insecurity, financial security and desire to maintain status quo, global insecurity, and fear of economic competition in the global market. Similarly, it is this era that American parents started overprotecting their children as well as dictating careers. They wanted their children to pursue careers regarded secure and lucrative rather than follow their creative dreams and potentials. In a research conducted by Kim which involved synthesizing empirical studies conducted between 1966 and 2008, various determiners of creativity experienced a decrease since the 1990s among them fluency, originality, elaboration, the abstractness of titles, creative strengths in Americans of all ages (Kim).

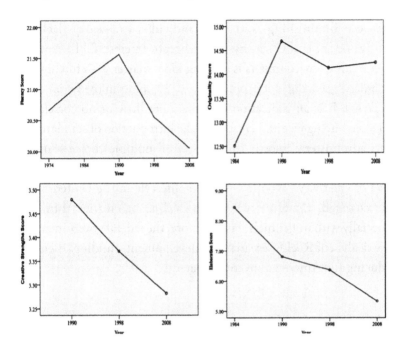

Charts showing a variation of various aspects of creativity (Kim)

According to Kim's research, the above-listed aspects of creativity have declined, but the biggest decline is experienced in Creative Elaboration (Kim). This is the aspect used for assessing the ability to own an idea and expand it in an interesting and novel way. The average Elaboration score on the Torrance Tests of Creativity Thinking between 1984 and 2008, for children from kindergarten through 12th grade was found to fall. It was indicated to decrease with more than one standard deviation, an indication that more than 85% of kids in 2008 scored lower on TTCT than the average kid in 1984 (Gray). Currently, the decline in creative thinking for younger kids is probably rampant at home rather than in schools, since first graders and kindergarteners appear to be influenced more while they are at home than school, the reason why research suggests the necessity of transferring creativity from art room to homeroom. Although the IQ score is known to increase worldwide, creativity has been diminishing, and many individuals nowadays lack the ability and skills of Curiosity, Preference, or Interest (CPI). Presence of enriching environments is making kids smarter with intelligence recorded to score up with approximately 10 points in the Flynn effect (Merritt). It is an indication that there lies little or no correlation between intelligence and creativity. The introduction of standardized tests administered mostly in the form of multiple-choice scantron tests, drive students to memorization and no longer assess their level of creativity (Woolsey). Besides, lifestyle in the United States has changed, therefore, causing a decline in creative thinking, especially with millennials. Furthermore, the federal government has drastically cut R&D (research and development) funding, therefore reducing the American inventor's patents.

Analysis of Issues Causing Creativity Decline in the United States

Every child is born creative and only require support and empowerment to put the imaginations into practice. Instead of cultivating the creativity, many schools drive it away since they concentrate on teaching numeracy and literacy. The argument that it is impossible to teach creativity to young children due to classroom workload can be regarded as a false trade-off. It is important to understand that creativity does not entail freedom from concrete facts but rather fact-finding as well as deep research (Westby). However, the current generation fails to understand this argument. In the United States, the belief seems to be deep-rooted since creativity is reported to continue declining whereas, in other nations like Germany, France, Switzerland, Netherlands, Singapore,

Belgium, United Kingdom and Ireland, creativity has continued to rise. In countries with declining creativity, there is a likelihood that children spend most of their time being taught artificial skills to enable the passing of exams. By the time they get into the job industry, they have been conditioned to conform to a specific way of thinking. In real facts, most schools in the current world are not designed to cultivate creativity, but to teach the 19th-century Prussian model. They aim at teaching students to obey rather than how to find solutions to challenges. Also, the message teachers are given from the environment outside the school is to teach the basics and enhance more discipline, something which has little impact on stimulating creative learning.

Over the years, children have lost curiosity and passions due to the incentives and sanctions in schools. Since the introduction of students' test scores, many schools have turned to rote lecturing, and they aim at teaching testable school curriculum as well as test-taking skills. Students memorize information, and there is little time to put it into practice. Instead of our bureaucratic education system raising us to meet every day challenges of the day, they are busy teaching kids on tests. Instead of advocating for "No Child Left Behind," they are literary leaving all American children behind and failing to prepare them to be creative humans (Chao). Today, we live in a world full of exponential complexity and ruthless competition. As years continue to pass, students continue to graduate, failing out, while others are dropping out of school, due to test-phobia, with no significant changes. Unfortunately, as a result, children have lost interest in coming up with ideas since the school curriculum was adopted. The rigid and formulaic educational system is just concentrating on training students in a specific path of doing things (Robinson). Although there is no perfect education system, the one used should however not dictate what students should do. It is heartbreaking that most of the problems affecting creativity appears in the system and not with the teachers. It is of serious concern that education systems are lacking the capacity to promote creativity, which is the only ability that differentiates humans from robots. Although teachers are always willing to promote and develop creativity among learners, even within the stiffing education systems, the guidelines provided by the current education systems act as a limitation.

The use of tests as a measure of success always bring competition among students and therefore narrow their visions and goals. In the past, the greatest of all innovators were inspired by big visions such as "zeal to change the world," empathy and compassion to find solutions to global challenges. Their expanded visions assisted their minds to transcend real constraints and limitations and recognize patterns existing among the unrelated. Around the 1980s, countries such as the USA, Australia, and the UK turned their attention to the development of theories and research aimed at enhancing education. Many of the theories and practices focused on the quality and quantity of instructions offered in schools which in turn enhanced students' outcomes (Creemers). Many of the schools by then had high expectations and provided solutions to daily challenges. However, in the 1990s, the school system was altered, and schools started to focus on scores. It was at this time that students started to be grouped as quick and slow learners. Two decades after the establishment of the new education system, there are significant changes which are reported to affect creativity. Among the issues associated with students of current days include low school expectations, avoidance of risk-taking, low collaboration, and narrowing of minds, fostering of conformity, fostering of hierarchy, and losing of imagination and deep thoughts (K. Kim).

Currently, schools are focusing on strategies which will only assist students to pass exams. In most cases, teachers focus more on students that score low in tests so that they can improve. They ignore the high-achieving students, therefore lowering their expectations, achievement as well as hard work. Also, high-stakes testing present in schools today scare away students, therefore influencing them to stop taking risks for fear of failing (K. Kim). In addition, the parents of today's world want their children to engage only in activities and tasks which are secure and less risky. It is worth understanding that willingness to fail is paramount for creativity. Today's education system is discouraging collaboration. Teachers have been compelled to utilize rote lecturing and therefore provide students with minimal time for discussions and group work. Since success is measured by individual performance on tests, many students opt to take studies on their own. Another common phenomenon entails a reduction of instruction time as well as the elimination of non-tested subjects. Subjects such as physical education, science, social studies, foreign language and arts which provide a student with an opportunity to expand mind are not provided in some of the schools. In schools where they are present, the instructional time awarded is reduced, therefore reducing the opportunities for students to find or express their prowess and know-how in those subjects. Similarly, the current education system is associated with children losing their imagination ability and deep thoughts. Test-centric education has minimized the playtime for children, which is known to cultivate imagination. Also, with the pressure to cover testable materials, teachers are forced to overfeed students with information, therefore leaving them with little thinking time or opportunity to explore concepts taught in depth (K. Kim). Moreover, the American education system and education systems for other countries experiencing a decline in creativity are fostering conformity. They teach students similar information and administer the same tests to them. These tests have comprised uniqueness and originality for learners and educators as it was before 1990. Children can no longer fulfill their creative potentials. Lastly, hierarchy refers to the structural inequalities present in the educational sector today. It is unfair to measure the intelligence of a child using tests since some of them started experiencing un-deservingness right from early childhood. In contrast, schools are using the high-stakes testing as a determiner of intelligence and the students who fail are blamed for their lack of effort (Linkner).

The greatest decline in creativity among the young American generation is an indication that they are more affected by the test-centric education in the nation. As stated earlier, a creativity crisis occurs when the ION (inbox, outbox, and newbox) Thinking skills and the 4S Attitude are affected (K. Kim). In such a case, they cause a decrease in the ability of children right from kindergarten through sixth grade come up with new ideas, therefore bringing up a few innovators. They play an essential role in cultivating innovators. Although other parts of the world are raising up innovators, America seems to continue killing their eagles. The trend is ranging from kindergarten through sixth grade. About the 4S Attitudes, creative attitude is regarded as the way in which people react to the artistic climate. The 4S attitudes which consist of soil, storm, sun, and space reflect the 4S climate. As Kim states, soil attitude such as open-mindedness, resourcefulness, biculturalism, and complexity-seeking are cultivated by the soil climate. On the other hand, the sun climate cultivates sun attitudes which include optimism, curiosity, big-picture-thinking, playfulness, and spontaneity. Similarly, there is the storm climate which nurtures storm attitudes such as diligence, independence, risk-taking, self-discipline, self-efficacy, persistence, resilience, and uncertainty-accepting. Lastly, there is the space climate which cultivates space attitudes. Among the aspects developed in space, climate include emotional expressiveness, self-reflection, autonomy, compassion, defiance, daydreaming, nonconformity, and gender-bias-free. The TTCT is used to measure playfulness, open-mindedness, emotional expressiveness, nonconformity, and daydreaming which are vital in determining creativity.

Open-minded attitude refers to the way in which individuals perceive other's views which appear contradictory to one's beliefs. It is an ability which develops in early childhood through exposing a child to early diverse life experiences and cultures. It is measured using resistance to closure subscale. Open-minded attitude allows an individual to play a vital role in nurturing innovators since they get exposed to a flexible way of life. Also, they learn how to be daring and open to interests and broad experiences such as imagination and fantasy. Furthermore, exposing individuals to a liberal attitude allows them to develop a culture of learning wherein they always get an improved understanding which enables them to develop critical thinking skills as well as expertise. Regarding emotional expressiveness, Americans have in recent years recorded low. This is a term used to refer to emotional attitudes among them understanding, expression, and recognition. Emotional expressiveness assists individuals in communicating their states of mind as well as empathy for others. It is an ability which every innovator should possess since it assists innovators to be emotionally expressive in sensitive environments. In many instances, emotions affect creativity more than cognitive or any other rational factors found in the creative realm. Before things started to change, Americans were ranked high concerning liberal attitude and emotional expressiveness. However, they began to decrease in the 1990s after test-centric education became dominant.

Also, the creativity crisis has been fueled by decreased playful attitude. Playfulness refers to the ability of people approaching situations in an exploratory manner. Also, it assists individuals in perceiving challenges in a lighter style. Innovators are people who are playful and keep focused on the goal. The energy they possess sustain them, and they always feel free to utilize their outbox thinking. They make use of proactive approaches which facilitate newbox thinking, therefore come up with ideas or solutions rarely thought using our common sense. Parents and children of current days fear to engage their minds in ambiguous and risky tasks, an indication of the cause of reduced unlocking of potential creativity. Similarly, the decline in daydreaming attitude within American has caused their ability to create. Daydreaming attitude refers to the sustenance of unrealistic but goal-oriented thoughts while an individual is awake. It is paramount in assisting people to capture useful aspects of cognition, which in turn benefit outbox and newbox thinking. It is a common phenomenon with a majority of innovators, allowing them to come up with unique ideas necessary for innovation. Furthermore, the current education system in the

United States has compromised nonconformity attitude. It refers to the ability of individuals to feel comfortable even in instances where they have deviated from the mainstream pattern of thoughts and behavior. Nonconformity is vital in assisting individuals to attain uniqueness beyond the existing norms. Before the 1990s, nonconformity assisted innovators to utilize their outside thinking and surpass the traditional way of thinking to come up with new approaches, concepts, and products. They were able to reject limits imposed by others, set their limits, and had the power to pursue their own goals. However, these ceased when the test-centric education system was introduced since it dictated specific goals which were to be achieved by all students passing through the system.

With the technological advancements currently witnessed worldwide, lifestyle has changed. Social media, the internet, televisions, computers have dominated the daily lives of Americans and kids nowadays spend more hours on them than engaging in creative activities (Brown). Nowadays, you will find children glued in front of the television, chatting with a friend via social media or playing video games. Also, the internet trains individuals to cultivate "followers," and "likes" and "views" even on things that impinge on our creative process. Also, a lot of information read by people on the internet is just opinions and lack scientific support, and the rate at which people "like" or "follow" it is heartbreaking. In schools, teachers are less concerned with nurturing creativity since they are always busy teaching testable materials. The standards set in the curriculum seem to overwhelm them and have on several occasions stated that the current educational system lacks the room for a creativity class. Kids are lucky if they get a single art class in a week, something Mark Runco from the University of Georgia terms as "art bias" (Bronson). With the current education system, students score low when subjected to create tasks, and in most cases, the scores show a standard deviation. It is an indication that the education system has corrupted their brains to the extent that they possess an almost similar way of thinking.

Introduction of test-centric education systems affected skillful thinking. Creative processes such as fluid thinking, flexible thinking, and primary outbox were affected, therefore causing a decline in the ION thinking skills. The fluid thinking was a skill used before the 1990s to create ideas impulsively. Generation of many ideas provided innovators with a variety; therefore, they had the freedom to come up with unique and more improved ideas. Since 1990, these skills were reduced, and therefore individuals started coming up with only strong ideas instead of generating many ideas. Similarly, the existence of flexible thinking was an added advantage to innovators since they could generate ideas from various angles. Also, the skill provided innovators with a variety of options when finding solutions to a problem. Currently, Rote learning trains students only on memorization and concentration on testable materials. All students are equipped with a specific way of thinking which is inherited from one age group to the other. Besides, rote learning and memorization have led to a reduction in fundamental thinking skill, and students can no longer formulate new or unusual ideas. It is among the critical elements of creativity but a change in behavior and practices due to status quo and social pressure have resulted in its decline in modern days.

As prior stated, newbox thinking is responsible for synthesizing, promotion and transformation of new ideas. Synthesizing can be termed as the process of recombining information into a new coherent form while maintaining the meaning of each part. Currently, the majority of Americans cannot synthesize information and ideas. They cannot come up with information bigger beyond what they can see. The current environment has transformed them into individuals who depend on boundary-crossed skills, and education certificates are used as the measure of intelligence. There is a likelihood that many cannot think beyond what they have been taught in schools and therefore rank very low regarding creative strengths. Similarly, only a few individuals in the current generation can utilize dot-connecting skills which occur as a result of perceiving things in improved perspectives (Myers). It is an indication that the majority of people in recent days cannot think metaphorically. They fear using their five senses to connect irrelevant information or things to come up with new ideas. It is a challenge in the current world which have made companies find alternatives ways of doing things such as the use of algorithms and robotics. These artificial synthesizers of information are also being used in the transformation process. Synthesized ideas require to be transformed into functional creations and therefore, there is always needing to have pursuit-of-simplicity skills which transform complex ideas into simple forms as well as remove destructors from an innovation. According to Amabile "... creativity gets killed [in mature companies] much more often than it gets supported... ...creativity is undermined unintentionally every day in work environments that were established--for entirely good reasons--to maximize business imperatives such as coordination, productivity, and control" (Solomon).

The change in lifestyle has also reduced the likelihood of promotions. In the past, it was common to find multiculturalism in big American cities. People from various regions, religions, ethnicities, sexual orientations, and cultures used to collaborate and share ideas. However, with the world being reduced to a global village due to technological advancements, promotions have been reduced. The likelihood of people coming together to discuss issues physically has reduced since many currently prefer using social media platforms. Besides, children are not exposed to storytelling, metaphors and nonverbal communication although they are helpful in the improvement of visualization and the five senses. Storytelling is an important practice which assists in crafting skills as well as memory. This is because it entails communication of information in a simplified and more persuasive way. Therefore, listeners can be able to create mental images as the narrator talk, and this is a great step in developing a creative mind.

Federal and State governments continue to slash funding meant for art and science. During the last four decades, state and federal governments have been allocating funds and supporting arts in 56 states (National Assembly of State Arts Agencies). Over time, however, this is changing since the government has reduced art funding during recessions. The cut is similar and has been done across all states in the nation. Some schools can no longer support art subjects such as music. As prior stated, creativity is mostly enhanced through science and art. Therefore, the cut has affected creativity. When the United States is slashing funds meant for subjects which enhance creativity, other nations such as Britain and China are implementing programs meant to enhance creativity. For instance, in 2008, the British secondary school curricula revamped from science to foreign languages with the aim of emphasizing idea generation. The European Union in 2009 held the European Year of Creativity and Innovation, which was aimed at promoting the neuroscience of creativity (ECOTEC). Also, there was the financing of teacher training as well as the introduction of problem-based learning programs for both children and adults. On the other hand, China has enrolled in universal educational reforms with the aim of eliminating the drill and kill teaching style. The schools are also adopting a problem-solving learning system.

Possible Ways of Regaining Creativity

Although creativity is perceived to decline, there is still room to cultivate it back. As prior stated, group work tends to limit creativity through social inhibition and cognitive interference. However, if well utilized, groups have the potential of improving creativity through processes of providing the right cognitive and social stimulations. There is the need for schools, government or organizations to create an environment with the right climate for creativity such as the teaching of creative problem-solving instead of rote memorization. Students benefit more when they learn strategies of reaching to the right choice and concepts than when they are taught on testable materials since they easily forget the learning material after taking the standardized test. Also, there is a need to train students to challenge assumptions instead of assimilating them the way they are presented. Creativity is all about imagining the possibilities instead of following a specific operating manual. Furthermore, parents and teachers should cease to be so protective and train children not to fear to make mistakes while learning. Mistakes are common while learning and eventually lead to a discovery.

The current education system is regarded as the primary contributor to the declined creativity. Therefore, teachers should be required to work harder and introduce programs which can promote a creative class mindset. It is a strategy which can allow children to be innovative in class and be creative in the future. If America continues depending on rule-following memorization instead of teaching critical thinking, there is a likelihood of other countries replacing as an economic superpower. It is time to empower Americans with critical ingredients necessary for creativity. Example of such include integrating arts whereby instead of treating various arts separately, they should be integrated to appear similar to traditional subjects such as math, science, and language. It is a strategy which can assist in reducing the tendency of learners memorizing testable materials and instead become active beyond class topics. Also, art integration can assist to bring back interest to learners, and their test scores improve as well as strengthen his or her attentiveness, comprehension and reaction time. According to researchers, it is easy for learners to recall and retain what they learn through arts integration than during standardized tests. Teachers also have a part to play to make the most of the arts learning in the classroom. Even without finances, teachers are capable and should find arts integration initiatives to use in their classrooms. They should try to come up with a themed learning model, which assist to reach out to other art teachers for purposes of partnering and sharing ideas. It is a strategy that can assist in bringing greater learning experiences in schools.

In conclusion, everybody has a part to play in bringing back creativity in schools as well as the nation. Since everyone is born with a creative mind, unlocking that potential can be useful in formulating programs and strategies which can assist in bringing up creative children. Parents should cease discouraging their children from engaging in activities regarded as 'insecure.' They should learn to encourage their children whenever they fail so that they can keep on trying. Similarly, parents and schools need to bring back storytelling since it played an essential role during the early years of child development. A child is best trained on doing things in a certain way right from kindergarten. If the government could alter the current education system to reduce test-centric learning, students and teachers could get time to engage in activities that enhance creativity. Also, parents and teachers need to train their kids in the best way of using the internet. They should be taught how to access or visit sites which offer information about research, creativity, and innovation. With all these, there is no doubt creativity can be regained.

HOW DYSLEXIA IS ADVANTAGEOUS TO ENTREPRENEURS

This may appear to be a perplexing chapter, but it hits home with me. I was lucky to have grown up in a loving and affluent family. From the outside, I was a bright and outgoing kid. However, school was a struggle for me and my parents. Athletically and socially I exceled, but in school I struggled. To my parents and my teachers, my struggles appeared to be from a lack of effort. It was in 8th grade that I took a standardized test to apply to an east coast prep school. When I scored in the bottom one percent of all Americans they thought I must have mixed up my answer tree. I took the same test again the following month with the same results. At this point my parents had some testing done only to find out that I was dyslexic. The results of the findings were that my parents couldn't blame my grades on my effort anymore, but I still needed a college education to get a good job. I found that the other side of my brain could get me my diploma from college. It was Art and Art History that got me through college. I didn't have a chance of passing all the traditional classes with final exams. My strategy was to get as many credits as I could in studio art classes and use my social skills to talk and charm my way through my art history classes. As long as I showed up to every class, sat in the front row, went to professor office hours and asked for help, the professors awarded me a passing grade. It worked! I received a BA from college and now it was off to the real world.

My only real qualifications were to be a starving artist. I figured that the world already had enough of them, so I opted to move to New York City and play the 'who you know game." Eventually one of my father's college fraternity brothers offered me a position on Wall Street.

I found out that I excelled at sales and marketing. I rose to the top quickly. I was always asked why I was so successful. In the beginning I didn't have the answer. My peers went to better schools and had better grades. These were some of the best and brightest kids, so why was I besting them and why were they interested in how I was doing things? A few years later I figured out what made me the leader. I thought differently. I was always searching better and different ways to communicate with my clients. I was thinking with the opposite side of my brain than the others. Why was I thinking that way? Because I couldn't compete trying to do things the traditional way. I couldn't comprehend reading materials. I couldn't grasp the analytics involved in what I was selling, but I could take a complicated subject matter and simplify it, so I could understand it, and more importantly my clients could understand it. I was humble enough to know that I couldn't comprehend the details, but had no problem finding bright people to help me understand it. To me, it was like the office hours with the professors in college. While my colleagues were trying to educate the consumers, I was figuring out the best way to market and communicate the simplified version to the clients. I owe my success to my ability to think differently. Because of my dyslexia, I learned to use the creative side of my brain. Now that I look back at my career, I owe much of my success to my learning disability.

It appears that I am not alone with my success. Julie Logan, emeritus professor of entrepreneurship at Cass Business School, in London, says that 35% of company founders in the United States identified themselves as dyslexic, compared with 15% in the general population. "Dyslexic entrepreneurs reported as good or excellent at oral communications, delegation, creative and spatial awareness tasks, whilst non-dyslexics reported as average or good," Logan says. As a dyslexic, I believe we have an advantage over non-dyslexics when it comes to problem solving, communication, delegation and creative skills. These are key traits when it comes to business founders and leaders.

Dyslexia, just like many other disorders have been portrayed in a bad light by society for the longest time. However, there seems to be growing evidence to suggest that dyslexics have a cutting edge with regards to business leadership and entrepreneurship. This is particularly true when considering the number of successful business leaders or entrepreneurs who have been diagnosed with dyslexia. Various definitions have been put forth to describe the disorder, but the most common one, that this discussion intends to use is to consider it as a reading disorder affecting people despite being with normal intelligence. The extent to which people are affected varies, in terms of portraying the most common symptoms such as difficulties in writing words, spelling as well as reading fast among many other challenges. In regard to having traits that are advantageous to business leadership and entrepreneurship, those with the condition often come along as excellent problem solvers, looking at things differently, excellent oral communicators and tend to rely on social cues and intuition. Scholars associates the aforementioned traits with those required for a person to succeed as a business leader or entrepreneur. The discussion thus intends to look at various advantages that dyslexics have that made them more successful as business people or as entrepreneurs. In addition, the discussion will provide various examples of how the condition has helped various leaders. In doing so, it would also be important to look at some qualities that make people succeed in business as leaders or entrepreneurs.

Qualities of Successful Entrepreneurs and Business Leaders

There are several traits that help people succeed as entrepreneurs or business leaders. Understanding these traits would help to make an informed judgment on whether people with dyslexia are at an advantageous or disadvantageous position as business leaders or entrepreneurs. First, to succeed in the two aspects, one must be a good communicator. This is especially true for business leaders. Communication has been described as the most vital skill a leader needs to have. The reason that makes the trait be of high significance is its ability to promote all other skills. Other benefits that come with communication include but are not limited to helping leaders resolve issues, promote sales, negotiate deals, rally employees or address the challenges facing their businesses or investors (Eide). In addition to communication, entrepreneurs know how the future might unfold which helps them make a wise long-term investment as opposed to short-term gains. To be a successful entrepreneur, a person's thinking must be several steps ahead of others as well as have a continuous thirst for emerging opportunities for development and growth. The mentality of being future-focused is critical for several reasons. First, it prevents a person from instant gratification to sacrifice for the benefits of the future. The willingness to embrace failure is another trait attributed to people who succeed as entrepreneurs. Successful entrepreneurs like to take risks and not afraid to fall or face any significant challenge that may be looming in their journey (Singh, and Habib). They consider failure as an opportunity for growth and would try to make the best choices when put in difficult situations. The ability to accept that things might not go as planned or turn out to be successful is critical for entrepreneurs. Therefore, they are more than ready to put into practice new ideas they consider essential. Lastly, creativity and innovation are one trait that nearly all entrepreneurs possess (Singh, and Habib). This is primarily to say that these people have the unwavering drive to continuously come up with new concepts or ideas as well as improve the existing ones.

Most entrepreneurs entered the business world by coming up with new ideas and as such, their creativity or innovativeness continue to shape their business. They like change and would readily welcome any change that promises to promote their productiveness and as a result, improve the production of goods and services (Singh, and Habib). The ability to solve problems, leadership skills, likeability as well as being able to make initiatives have been associated with successful business leaders. Most traits mentioned have also been associated with people suffering from dyslexia, and as such, it is often believed the condition predisposes them to be successful business leaders and entrepreneurs. For this reason, it is worth discussing what are some of the advantages dyslexic people have that makes scholars believe as such.

How Dyslexia Stand to Benefit Entrepreneurs and Business Leaders

There are several qualities common to dyslexics that are good for business leadership or entrepreneurship. First, dyslexics happen to have high emotional quotient as well as being people-centric (Eide). That is to say that these people like working in teams. They not only prefer groups but have personalities that are great for the working environment in addition to team building. They can identify people who can make a great team, work with them in establishing a good working environment where each is committed to promoting the agenda of the group. A high emotional quotient, on the other hand, develops their listening skills and empathy. The two qualities are great for business leaders as well as for entrepreneurs since it promotes loyalty among employees and customers because the leader can not only listen to what they want but also align the business to match with employee and customer demands (Eide). The two qualities of dyslexics are tremendous and stand to benefit business leaders and entrepreneurs. Also, it is for this reason that one would argue that dyslexia condition is advantageous for business leaders and entrepreneurs.

The ability to communicate well is another quality that is common with dyslexics and which is good for business leaders and entrepreneurs. Studies on dyslexic's communication abilities show that most of them are great communicators and as such, can articulate the vision of the company in a way that will make people follow the same vision (Eide). This group of people is unique regarding how they communicate in the sense that they can paint a picture by use of words while communicating. In business, communication is key for leaders, as it helps to resolve issues arising at the workplace, helps in negotiations, helps as a tool to motivate employees and lastly, helps relay information to investors and customers. Therefore, communication helps dyslexics win the confidence of customers, investors, and employees, which makes them great business leaders and entrepreneurs (Eide).

Strong metacognition is another trait that is common among people with the dyslexia condition. This is according to research carried out on college students. One would describe metacognition as the ability of a person to be aware of his or her thinking mechanisms. They are therefore able to use what they learn from their thinking processes to their advantage or for the benefit of the business. One of the most important results that those with high metacognition ability demonstrate is their ability to delegate tasks to the most suitable person (Eide). This stems from self-awareness in the sense that a person can appreciate the fact that he or she cannot excel at all tasks and as such, it would be wise to delegate the same to specific individuals who are most qualified and highly talented. This is important in many ways. Firstly, it helps build a strong team, and secondly, it ensures that startups do not fail because of failure to delegate responsibilities to the most suitable members (Eide). Dyslexics are regarded as people with high tendency to hire talented individuals or build strong teamwork. All these aspects are beneficial to both business leaders and entrepreneurs.

One of the essential traits that entrepreneurs and to some extent business leaders must have is innovativeness or creativity. The business world and customer demand are ever changing, and therefore, it is the responsibility of business leaders as well as entrepreneurs to come up with new ideas that would satisfy the ever-changing customer or market demands. For entrepreneurs, in particular, it is hard to even consider yourself as such without being creative or innovative. Research carried out on people who have dyslexia reveals that they tend to be highly creative or innovative (Bowers). Their innovativeness and creativity help them not only start a business but also stay afloat despite the dynamics existing in the marketplace. They are thus able to come up with new ideas that would help the business grow or prevent their startup from failing. These aspects make dyslexic extremely good as entrepreneurs and business leaders. For this reason, people with dyslexia can be in advantageous position with regards to business leadership and entrepreneurship.

There are other traits in addition to the ones mentioned above that makes people suffering from dyslexia to be at an advantageous position for business leadership and entrepreneurship than non-dyslexic individuals. First, the condition hinders their academic and learning abilities, therefore exposing them to failure at a very early stage of life. Studies show that their failure in schools has a double positive effect, in particular, in the development of other skills as well as being familiar with failure (Jackson). One of the traits that they develop is a keen sense of problem-solving, which is useful in business. Regarding failure, they don't fear failure and thus are willing to try new things. They put into practice new ideas despite the risk associated with ideas not always turning out as successful as initially envisioned (Gladwell, 124). The ability to tolerate adversity is good both for business leaders and entrepreneurs. Therefore, it would not be that crazy to argue that dyslexia is good for business leadership and entrepreneurship.

The discussion regarding dyslexia as a beneficial condition to business leaders and entrepreneurs has thus demonstrated various traits similar to the one required for people to succeed as business leaders and entrepreneurs. Although, society in general, has not been friendly to dyslexics, it needs to start shifting that kind of mentality and treat them with as much respect as other people, mainly because they have great potential in business leadership and entrepreneurship. The link between dyslexia and entrepreneurship or business leadership is what makes these people better than non-dyslexics (Eide). For that reason, it is essential to look at how the condition has helped some business leaders.

Dyslexia and Successful Business Leaders or Entrepreneurs

Richard Branson is one of the most successful business leaders and entrepreneurs the world over. The CEO of Virgin is known to be dyslexic and attributes the condition to his successes as a business person. According to Branson, dyslexia made him struggle at school which in turn, made teachers, as well as his fellow learners, believe that he was either stupid or lazy (Snyder). However, he argues that the condition should not worry many who are affected, as they can use it to their advantage. For instance, Branson states that the condition helped him learn to delegate the tasks he was not good at to the most suitable people available within his organization. The businessman further argues that delegating the tasks reduced the responsibilities he was assigned, thus allowing him to focus on the bigger picture of how to expand his business empire (Snyder). For that reason, the condition helped him to be one of the most successful businessmen, expanding his business to different countries across the globe. This demonstrates how dyslexia helped Richard Branson.

Barbara Corcoran is a successful real estate mogul who is featured on the TV reality show known as 'Shark Tank.' She also acknowledges the fact that she is dyslexic, but argues that the condition was highly beneficial to her success as a real estate investor. She argues that the condition was instrumental in making her more competitive, social and creative than she imagined she could be without being dyslexic (Snyder). She thus encourages people suffering from the condition not to label themselves as a failure due to the schooling system which is largely disadvantageous to the dyslexic. According to her, the grading system in schools does not help bright students since they are not exposed to challenges which explains why they do not become as successful in life (Snyder). The schooling system thus conditions bright students not to be as successful as entrepreneurs. This illustrates how she credits her condition as a great influencer to her success in real estate.

John Chambers who was the head of Cisco once opened up about his dyslexia condition and as such, decided to be an advocate for the condition. According to the former CEO, he struggled in both third and fourth grade to the extent his teachers were doubting whether he would make it to college (Snyder). However, Chambers believes the condition helped him be more efficient in solving problems than he could have been without the condition. He believes that due to the condition, he is now able to arrive at solutions faster by eliminating problems or doing away with what does not seem to be right (Snyder). Like Branson and Corcoran, John Chambers believes that dyslexia helped him be more successful.

The final dyslexic business leader for this discussion is Paul Orfalea. Orfalea is known for being the founder of a copying behemoth, formally known as Kinkos. He was not a bright student owing to the condition but would, in turn, use his condition to his advantage. Orfalea states that he would always prefer to hire people who did not have his skills to carry out tasks he intended to perform (Snyder). According to him, A students would put a lot of effort for excellence while the C student would question the effort and the result. He believes that his condition helped him learn how to get the more skilled persons to carry out the duties on his behalf (Snyder). Dyslexia should thus not be viewed in the bad light because Paul Orfalea argues that it can help a person discover a hidden potential or an alternative way of doing things. Paul, like many other leaders, demonstrates how the condition has helped him as a business person, which can also apply to other business leaders or entrepreneurs despite society not expecting much from them. The evidence of the importance of dyslexia condition further underscores the advantages of the condition for business leaders as well as entrepreneurs.

In Conclusion

Dyslexia is a disorder that hinders a person from achieving academic excellence despite one being intelligent. However, as demonstrated in the above discussion, scholars are finding associations between qualities that help people succeed as entrepreneurs or business leaders and those possessed by people with dyslexia. Success in business and entrepreneurship has been attributed to good communication, building an effective team, taking risks, being able to solve and foresee problems, innovativeness, and creativity as well as withstanding adversity. People with dyslexia have shown to possess most of these qualities. Most of them are highly creative, are more willing to take risks, do not worry of failure since they are used to adversity and lastly, they come along as people who like delegating tasks. All these traits are ideal for both business leadership as well as entrepreneurship. Some successful leaders have come forth to stress how this condition and its traits are useful for their journey to success as a business person. The discussion has looked at Richard Branson, Barbara Corcoran, John Chambers and lastly, Paul Orfalea, all of whom have credited the condition for helping them as business persons.

POSITION YOUR SELF

As brilliant an "out-of-the-ordinary" thinker and doer you are, now it is time to implement. A brilliant idea and innovation go nowhere without the art of "positioning." How will you be positioning in the minds of your clients and prospects? The key to this chapter is to learn how to position yourself, your firm and your products in the mind of the advisor.

We need to understand the world of communication in our business. While we live in a world of over communication, very little communication takes place. We just throw a lot of noise at the consumers but fail to communicate a very simple strategy to position ourselves in the consumer's mind. The battle is not for selling all our wonderful products to the clients, but the battle is for a place in their minds. You will never sell much until you get yourself positioned properly in their minds.

There is a timeless book called *Positioning: The Battle for Your Mind* written by Al Reis and Jack Trout. Every wholesaler should own this book. It does a wonderful job of explaining the many ways to position yourself, your products and your firm in the minds of the advisor.

In the book, Reis and Trout write:

> "In our over communicated society, the paradox is that nothing is more important than communication. With communication going for

you, anything is possible. Without it, nothing is possible. No matter how talented and ambitious you may be.

What's called luck is usually an outgrowth of successful communication. Saying the right things to the right person at the right time. Finding what the NASA people in Houston call a window in space.

Positioning is an organized system for finding a window in the mind. It is based on the concept that communication can take place at the right time and under the right circumstances."

I felt so strong about the idea of positioning and "winning the battle for the advisor's mind" that every day I remind myself that it was all about positioning. Just like a golfer who thinks about a couple of things before they start their swing. Just like a skier visualizing their run before starting. I use positioning to trigger my day. How could I position myself in the mind of my consumer?

In Reis and Trout's book they talk about "repositioning the competition." They write:

With a plethora of products in every category, how does a company use advertising to blast its way into the mind? The basic underlying marketing strategy must be "reposition the competition."

In other words, to move a new idea or product into the mind, you must first move an old one out.

Many years ago, Tylenol was trying to gain market share in the aspirin space. The market was dominated by power houses such as Anacin, Bayer, Bufferin and Excedrin. How could they reposition all those heavy weights? The solution was quite simple; they needed to reposition the entire aspirin marketplace.

According to Reis and Trout:

> Tylenol went out and burst the aspirin bubble.
>
> "For the millions who should not take aspirin," said Tylenol's ads. If your stomach is easily upset… or you have an ulcer… or you suffer from asthma, allergies, or iron-deficiency anemia, it would make good sense to check with your doctor before you take aspirin."
>
> "Aspirin can irritate the stomach lining," continued the Tylenol ad, "trigger asthmatic or allergic reactions, cause small amounts of hidden gastrointestinal bleeding."
>
> "Fortunately, there is Tylenol…"
>
> Sixty words of copy before any mention of the advertiser's product.
>
> Sales of Tylenol acetaminophen took off. Today Tylenol is the No. 1 brand of analgesic. Ahead of Anacin. Ahead of Bayer. Ahead of Bufferin. Ahead of Excedrin. A simple but effective repositioning strategy did the job.
>
> Against an institution like aspirin. Amazing.

I would like to share some of my firm, product and personal positioning ideas I used over the years with great success. Here is a repositioning strategy that was very useful in my ability to gather new clients at Fidelity Advisors, one on my past employers. I had just taken over a territory that ranked about 15th among all wholesalers in the Broker/Dealer channel, considered a middle of the road ranking within the unit. When I first got in the field I realized there was a strong dislike for Fidelity. The underlying distain was because the advisor viewed Fidelity as a competitor. Not only were they considered a competitor, but they believed that they were taking their clients. I needed to reposition our firm in their minds.

I needed to be able to show that we, like our competitors in the advisor distribution business, had the ability to grow their business. After thinking how Tylenol was able to reposition themselves in the marketplace, I needed to find a way to reposition our firm and products in the mind of our prospects. While working for Fidelity Investments I represented their mutual funds and retirement plans to the financial advisors at firms like Merrill Lynch, Morgan Stanley, Wells Fargo, UBS, LPL, and others. It was true that many of the advisor's clients and prospects were doing mutual fund business at Fidelity without using the financial advisors. Fidelity was viewed as a competitor to the financial advisors. Instead of sticking my head in the sand, I used their fears as an opportunity to reposition Fidelity in their minds and, at the same time, grow their business.

I started every meeting with an attention grapping line. I would say "Your customers are going to do business with Fidelity whether you like it or not." I continued, "Are they going to do it through you or someone else?" I had repositioned how they felt about Fidelity. They went from avoiding Fidelity like the plague to embracing the idea that I could help them take assets from Fidelity Investments branches.

Once they realized that their clients were thrilled that they could get Fidelity funds from their advisor they started to prospect with Fidelity. That repositioning strategy took me from the middle of the pact to the top three and earned me an annual invitation to the firms "Leadership Club."

Another example of how I used *Positioning* by Ries and Trout is how I started selling a product that had $0 in sales when I took over a territory for Nations Funds, the Bank of America Asset Manager. They had acquired a great money manager from Janus Capital a year earlier. His track record was sparkling, but people thought that he was too aggressive for their clients. He ran a concentrated portfolio style that was very different from the larger more popular funds that held over 100 names in their portfolios. The competitor's funds were very successful. Even though we had a superior track record the advisor was not happy with what they were holding. I needed a way to get them to consider using my manager, Tom Marsico.

I went back to the book by Reis and Trout and found an interesting positioning strategy. They talked about the Cola industry and how 7-Up found success in the soda world.

"Another classic positioning strategy is to worm your way onto a ladder owned by someone else, as 7-Up did. The brilliance of this idea can only be appreciated when you comprehend the enormous share of mind enjoyed by Coke and Pepsi. Almost two out of every three soft drinks consumed in the United States are cola drinks. By linking the product to what was already in the mind of the prospect, the "un-cola" position established 7-Up as an alternative to a cola drink. (The three rungs on the cola ladder might be visualized as: One, Coke. Two, Pepsi, and three, 7-Up.)" What 7-Up had done was to reposition itself into another space. In the mind of the soda drinker they had just given them an alternative to the colas that they have been drinking. They had opened an entirely new market place. In the minds of the drinkers, there were the cola brands such as Coke, Pepsi, Rite and all the other brown colas. 7-Up started a marketing strategy of the "un-cola." They wanted the consumer to know that there was more to the Soda market than Coke and Pepsi. It worked. Americans started to try the alternative un-cola. Their sales went through the roof. Since the soda drinkers have found the un-cola market soft drinks have exploded. Following 7-Up into the new space were drinks like Snapple and Gatorade. Now there is Red Bull and other power drinks. Without the "un-cola" campaign, who knows where the soft drink business would be today? Maybe it would still be only Coke and Pepsi.

I took this strategy and applied it to my product versus the competition. I decided that I needed to reposition the fund into its own space. I needed the advisor to open their mind to another idea. I went out and explained to the clients that our "growth fund" was very different from the ones that they were using. I explained that the other growth funds were the colas of the mutual fund business.

I then told them that there was an alternative market for growth investors. I called our product the "un-fund." I wanted to open their minds to the world of concentrated portfolios.

It worked. I took a new product with $0 sales in my territory to over $250 million in sales the first year. I used that strategy and continued to grow my sales every year. During that period, I was the top producer, net and gross, for seven years.

There are so many ways to position your firm, your products and yourself. You need a positioning strategy. Look outside the box to other industries and businesses. A simple strategy can catapult your sales to new heights. What is your positioning strategy?

OUT-OF-THE-ORDINARY BUSINESS LEADERS

Believe in yourself

Steve Jobs is considered one of the modern time influential and successful leaders in the world. Through his leadership and innovation, Steve has revolutionized mobile devices, music, and computers which have impacted our lives. Apple was formed in 1997 by Steve Wozniak and Steve Jobs and through the leadership of the latter, the company has transformed to become one of the most successful companies in the 21st century. Throughout his career, Steve Jobs made critical decisions and most current leaders look up to him and his style of leadership for inspiration. He understood the market, took into consideration the needs of the people and that helped him change the fate of Apple at the time of his demise. There are a lot of lessons that can be learned from Steve Jobs who was an influential and inspiring entrepreneur and leader.

One of the great decisions made by Steve Jobs that made Apple become more successful was choosing to outsource production to China. Apple moved its production to Asia as a strategy to lower its production costs and increase its revenue margin (Denicolai 342). Apple products were previously designed and produced in California and due to the high costs, the management of Apple was faced with the challenge of reducing costs and meeting the needs of the clients.

The decision by the tech giant was approved by Steve and despite the opposition from people and the federal government of the United States, the company went ahead and outsourced its production. The decision has had a long-term benefit for the company as it was able to reduce the production costs thus helping it to reduce the cost of products. The financial status of the company has improved ever since and most of the accolades have been directed to Steve Jobs who had strategically steered the company.

The second out of the box decision by Steve Jobs his choice of pursuing new innovative products. Before the return of Steve Jobs as the CEO, Apple was ailing and had lost its sparkle that made the future of the company to look bright. On his return, new products such as iMac, OS X, and the iPod were developed and released to the market. Steve Jobs saw the vision of future devices and convinced the company to focus on these innovative products. The sales of the company improved greatly, and Apple was able to compete against established companies in the space such as IBM and Microsoft. The company continues to develop these products and they have become popular in the United States and other parts of the world. The innovative products helped Apple from sinking into oblivion and making it be one of the most successful technology companies in modern history.

Another out of the box thinking by Steve Job was choosing to focus on fewer products. Steve was ousted after a boardroom coup which saw him losing his job at Apple and he went ahead and formed NEXT. The boards then acquired NEXT in 1997 and eventually made Steve Job as the CEO. The company had over time chose to invest in diverse products and that was not working well for them. As the new CEO, Steve changed the focus of the company to concentrate on 10 products as opposed to 350 products. With more concentration in fewer products, the company was able to create quality products that were appreciated by the people. The decision made the brand of the company grow and make more people realize their dreams. His vision for the company made the company more successful and his impact can still be felt, and Steve Jobs continues to be one of the most iconic businessmen in the modern era.

Out of His Mind?

Richard Branson is the brain behind the Virgin Group which is a conglomerate of businesses. The brand is behind business ventures such as hotels, an airline, transport, and radio among others. The conglomerate on average generates revenue of over $20 billion annually and employs over 70,000 people around the globe. The group was founded by Richard Branson and Nik Powell in 1970 and has over the years grown to be one of the most successful companies in the world. Through the stewardship of Branson, the company has grown from a startup and it currently helps other entrepreneurs set their foot in the market and thus give them an opportunity to make a change. Branson has over time encouraged people and leaders to make one-way decisions rather than two-way decisions and that is after a careful evaluation of the decision over a period.

One of the decisions made by Richard Branson that makes me consider him creative and a leader was the launching of Virgin Atlantic. Branson had been an exceptional leader in and revolutionized the music industry. He took a big leap as he ventured into the airline industry with little resources or experience and no guarantee of success. Virgin Records was sold for a whopping $1 billion which gave an opportunity for Richard Branson to venture into another businesses (Parker 889). It was a big risk to venture into the airline industry due to the competition and the initial cost of setting up the business. This decision showed that he was a decisive leader and was ready to take the risk in whatever direction the business went, and willing to learn from the mistakes. Virgin Atlantic has transformed to be one of the best airlines in the world and it has over the years become more successful.

The second key decision made by Richard Branson was deciding to go from the magazine business and venture into music. He had started the magazine business at age sixteen with the aim of using it as a tool to help the youths become to the next generation leaders. By being flexible and pivoting to another territory, the entrepreneur became more successful in the music business and that gave him the strength to venture into other industries. According to Niphadkar, the sale of Virgin records was one of the toughest business decisions Richard Branson has ever made in his career (543). If Branson had chosen to remain in the magazine business, he would have gone under within a short time as there was no cash flow in the venture. The Virgin Group which later became a force to reckon with more successful due to the quality leadership offered by Richard Branson.

Another key decision made by Richard Branson was venturing into the fuzzy drinks business. In 1994, Virgin Cola was launched into the market and it was meant to disrupt the industry that was dominated by Coca-Cola. Through his leadership, the Virgin Group had succeeded in disrupting other industries and it was for that reason that the company believed they could take on an established company such as Coca-Cola. The business was not successful. Richard Branson has declared that the failure made him make better decisions in future ventures. As a leader, mistakes are meant to make us learn and prepare us for the battles in the future and it was the reaction and decision of Branson that makes him an inspirational leader. Despite being successful, the failure was a great learning experience that has shaped him to be better and a more successful person in the modern world.

Changing the Way We Communicate

The current CEO and founder of Facebook are admired by many people as one of the most influential leaders. Facebook transformed from being a university social site to be the most successful social network in the whole world. Led by the CEO, the company has made many critical decisions which continue to make the company stand out and continue to be prosperous.

Zuckerberg has relied on people, purpose, and passion to make decisions and take risks in his pursuit to being successful. Facebook has revolutionized the way people communicate and spread information and the success of the company have been associated with the creative decisions of Mark Zuckerberg.

One key decision made by Mark Zuckerberg is the decision not to sell the company. According to Best, Zuckerberg was offered $5, $75 and $1 billion to sell the company at different stages of its existence (Best 22). Money is usually a distraction to many leaders and entrepreneurs. The choice to sell the company would have been the biggest regret for Zuckerberg as its current value is close to hitting the billion-dollar mark in the New York stock exchange.

Making such a choice shows that Zuckerberg was focused on building a long-term project and he believed in the project he was creating. The money would have been a distraction and making the decision, Mark Zuckerberg would not have been an influential leader as he is currently. Being young at the time, the money offered would have easily persuaded him but nonetheless, he chose to stick and believe in his vision. That is a critical lesson for any modern-day leader and entrepreneur and that shows how Zuckerberg is an out of the box thinker.

The second key decision made by Mark Zuckerberg was choosing to venture into the social network business. The project was first based in the university and Facebook had already dominated that space. The decision to scale and incorporate all people in the social network was a critical one and risky. Considering that companies such as Orkut had ventured and established itself in the market, Zuckerberg saw the gaps that needed to be filled and used the opportunity as the foundation for scaling the company. The foresight and belief that Facebook could become the biggest company in this space shows the great qualities that Zuckerberg portrays. Facebook, when it was a University project, was not making money and making the decision to scale was challenging. With factors such as internet not easily available, people did not own mobile devices and marketing done using conventional means, the company risked losing it all. Currently, Facebook is one of the biggest social network companies with over one billion active users spanning from around the world.

Another key decision made by Mark Zuckerberg was the announcement of making Facebook a platform. The company had been focusing on innovation and creating products that directly impact the lives of people. The expansion of the company into a platform has enabled Facebook to thrust to become more sustainable and successful. The rapid growth that has been achieved by the company has been because of believing in the improvements they make in a move to ensure Facebook continues to be prosperous. One key decision was the purchase of Instagram and through the leadership of Mark Zuckerberg, the company has acquired more clients and provides an alternate revenue stream for Facebook. The company continues to position itself as the market leader in changing the way people interact, advertise and share experiences in today's world. Such strategic decisions that have been made by Mark Zuckerberg is what makes him exceptional and he continues to inspire other people to pursue their dreams.

Rebel with a cause

Mark Cuban is one of the most successful serial entrepreneurs in the United States and around the world. His creativity and decisions have made him become successful and to be considered a modern-day leader. Initially, he ventured in technology and broadcast businesses but currently has invested in different sectors including sports and hospitality industries. When carefully analyzing the decisions made by Mark Cuban, two things stand out are his resilience and willingness to take risks. His first ventures were trials but over time, he transformed them to become bigger. The decisions he made were out of the box and overtime have paid off.

One of the critical business decisions made by Mark Cuban was moving to Dallas and creating a consulting company. Mark Cuban started out as a bartender but later created Micro Solutions. The technology business at that time was lucrative due to the demand by the people. It was a risk of creating a company in a new region with little experience. If Cuban had chosen to remain a bartender, the story would be different today. The company over time transformed from a small business to a big venture worth over $6 million. A lot of this achievements came after he created the company and sold it. The sale of his company paved the way for him to venture into other businesses and his creativity has made him to be considered one of the modern-day great business leaders in the world.

The second critical business decision made by Mark Cuban was creating AudioNet. After selling Micro Solutions, Cuban partnered with Tony Wagner to create an online radio that met the needs of the population. The company broadcasted shows and popular events acquiring more audience within a short period of time. The decision to venture into the online radio business was risky as people were still used to the conventional radio that broadcasted specific content. Later, the company ventured into video and music retailing, making it become even more popular in the United States market. Being passionate about technology, Cuban had made a mark for himself in the technology world. The radio and online businesses were a new venture, those added risk which meant; he could have lost a lot of resources. For over five years, Cuban and his partner continued developing the company and it became the best, despite others trying to venture into the business. His resilience and creativity finally paid off after the stock price of the company shot up, making him an instant billionaire.

Another critical business decision made by Mark Cuban was taking AudioNet public. According to an article by Business Insider, the stock prices of AudioNet which rebranded to bracdcast.com made in IPO history as its stock price jumped high on the first day (Drake, "Business Insider"). A total of over 2.5 million shares were sold at $74 while initially, they went for $18.

That was the instant Mark Cuban became a billionaire and the decision made him one of the most influential leaders in the modern era. Cuban then went ahead to sell his company for $6 billion dollars making the deal one of the most lucrative at the time. The decision by the leader shows his creativity and out of the box thinking. He created a company from scratch and went ahead to transform it into a billion-dollar company. Judging by his decision, it shows the kind of resilience and risks the leader was willing to take and it finally paid off. Through his decisions, the doors to more opportunities have opened and Mark Cuban continues to be an inspiration to young and old leaders today.

Changing the Way We Shop

Jeff Bezos who is the founder and current CEO of Amazon has been a great leader and an inspiration to many. The company he founded in 1994 first started as an online bookstore and has over time transformed to be the biggest e-commerce company in the world.

His creative decisions continue to have a major impact on his business and the lives of people around the world. His style of leadership shows he is a risk taker and loves to embrace change. Jeff Bezos has made critical decisions over the years and they have helped to transform Amazon to be worth over $1 trillion. His willingness to learn and commitment continues to make him an exceptional leader.

One of the key decisions made by Jeff Bezos is increased spending despite more risks emerging. Amazon has over the years ventured into different businesses some of which have been successful while others have failed. The smartphone business for instance failed and the company lost billions of dollars in the process. Likewise, some of the gambles taken by Amazon have paid off with ventures such as creating a data center and Kindle tablets being successful. Jeff Bezos has been vocal in explaining why the company makes bold moves to invest in risky ventures and he has received criticism from some quarters. The company is planning to invest more in the future in areas such as gas, technology, and manufacturing of products that are going to be sold throughout the world. Making such decisions continues to make Amazon successful as without taking the risks, the company in a short time will have to make hasty decisions in their quest to remain relevant in the competitive market.

The second key decision made by Jeff Bezos is choosing to create the Amazon Web Service business. Amazon built AWS as a good alternative to expensive in-house applications that were limiting and non-scalable (Irani 228). Through the leadership of Jeff Bezos, the company has chosen to make decisions that will satisfy the needs of their clients rather than focus on what the competitors are doing. The number of transactions being conducted in a day on Amazon has been rising and that creates a gap for a platform that can be scaled and can handle a lot of data. Better services would not be achieved if the company chose to continue relying on other companies' products. Other companies such as Walmart have been investing in this space and without providing better services, the company will be on the losing end. The AWS services are currently worth over $10 billion, and it continues to help meet the needs of Amazon clients.

Another key decision made by Jeff Bezos was starting Amazon and later diversifying the company operations. Jeff Bezos created Amazon to be an online bookstore after leaving his job as a software engineer (Kantor 77). The company at the beginning was selling books but later diversified to sell other products. Amazon currently is the biggest e-commerce company in the world with a worth of over $1 trillion. Through the leadership of Bezos, the company has scaled over the years and it continues to grow. Making the decision to sell other products shows the creativity and vision Bezos had for the company. From selling books, the company now sells a variety of products ranging from food, electronics, and movies among others. The company continues to invest in different products and Jeff Bezos continues to greatly support his move of investing in research and development. His leadership has been transformational for the company as they have led to growth and greatly impacts the lives of people in America and around the world.

Battery Man

Elon Musk is an adventurous and innovative entrepreneur who started by venturing into the computing business. He has been behind the success of brands such as PayPal, Tesla, Zip2 and Solar City among others. The entrepreneur has over time made critical decisions that have helped to steer forward companies that he has invested in and thus become more successful.

His success displays his brilliance and creativity he shows in the making of critical business decisions. One of the key business decisions made by Elon Musk is forming the Zip2 company. Elon Musk started the business in 1995 in partnership with his brother and a mutual friend. Zip2 started as a web software company that offered the city guide to newspapers in the United States (Matthews 27). The company was later acquired by Compaq computers in 1999 for $307 million and that was the start of the successful journey of Elon Musk. The vision for starting the company began while attending Stanford University and chose to defer to school to chase his dream. Elon Musk made a risky decision as the business was not guaranteed to work and that would have affected his life in the long term. Through the leadership of Elon Musk, the company was able to grow and be a million-dollar company. By creating a solution to a problem, newspaper companies were facing, Elon Musk was able to grow the company and show how creative he was as a leader.

The second key decision made by Elon Musk was investing in

Tesla Motors. The company was formed in 2003 and the aim of the company was creating affordable electric cars. Currently, in the modern world, people appreciate products that aim at conserving the environment thus ensuring the world will be a sustainable place. Tesla aimed to revolutionize the automotive industry and the positive impact it created has made the company and Elon Musk the CEO to receive accolades. In the initial stages, Tesla was just an idea and Elon Musk made a tough decision to invest in a product where the reception was; people were not yet determined. The company has over time transformed with one of its products. The 'Model S' becoming the world's best electric car in 2016. The demand for Tesla products has been on the rise in the United States and around the world and the value of the company continues to increase every day. Investing in the early stages of the company was one of the best decisions Elon Musk has ever made.

Another key decision made by Elon Musk was choosing not to cash out in the sale of Tesla Stock. According to an article by Eric Rosenbaum, in 2010, Elon Musk had run out of cash after investing all his money in Tesla (Eric, "CNBC"). The entrepreneur was able to live off loans from his friends and avoided the situation of selling some of his stock in Tesla. The options for this leader was limited and he had to make a tough decision that put him in a dilemma. The quick sale of his stock would not have made any financial sense and it was wise that Elon Musk stood by his position of avoiding selling his stocks. The current value of the stock in Tesla is worth more now, verification that he made the right decision. That dilemma is what many businessmen face and, in most instances, some will choose to sell the stake in their hard-developed businesses. The decision for not cashing out the Tesla stock shows again, how Elon Musk is a creative and out of the box thinker who inspired many people in the modern world.

We All Love Mickey Mouse

Walt Disney is a leader and entrepreneur who changed the animation industry through his creative work. The creativity and decisions made by Walt Disney are what many claim to be the basis behind the success of the company. The company has gone ahead and created quality contents that have been appreciated by diverse people in the world. Despite his demise, Walt Disney continues to be successful and the achievements have been attributed to the critical decision the founder made during his career.

One of the ways Walt Disney displayed creativity in his leadership was his continuation of working on Snow White. Walt Disney was discouraged by his wife and brother, who wanted to stop working on Snow White halfway through the project, due to lack of funds (Joel, "Addicted to Success"). The entrepreneur chose to stick by his decision and continued believing in his vision. He traveled with the aim of getting a producer who would fund his project. On completion of the project, Snow White received a standing ovation and it was through his decision that he was able to save his studio. This project is what made Disney famous and was the start of the successful journey of Walt Disney. The success he achieved came after he decided not to let obstacles be a hindrance to achieve his dreams. Looking at his dilemma, if the same had happened to most people, they would have cashed out or neglected the project. The decision made by Walt Disney was a turning point for his career and a new one for the world of animation.

The second way Walt Disney displayed creativity in his leadership was creating Disneyland and Walt Disney World. The idea of creating a theme park came from Walt Disney and the first park was built in 1955. The vision of the leader was to change the lives of the people through entertainment. The theme parks created by Disney has transformed to be the largest in the world and attracts millions of people annually. The company has over the years created more theme parks in the United States and other parts of the world and the parks are one of the major sources of revenue for Disney. Although Walt died before the opening of the second park, his vision has been embraced and continues to be enjoyed. The parks gave the company an alternative source of revenue and enabled it to connect with the younger generations who are the most vital market for the animation products. Through the creativity and strategic leadership of Walt Disney, the company has continued to grow, and it has been one of the most successful companies in the 20th and 21st century.

Another way Walt Disney displayed creativity in his leadership was choosing not to sign new contracts under Universal Studios. According to Lillestol, budget cuts made Walt Disney not to heed to the demands of Universal Studios who were the distributor of Walt Disney cartoons (Lillestol 231). The poor relationship between the two parties is what led to the development of Mickey Mouse which went ahead to become the most famous cartoon character. The budget cuts would have meant the quality of the animations by Walt Disney would have been reduced, due to the loses of his team. His decision paid off as he went ahead and created a company that became more successful. If Walt had chosen to stay and work under Universal Studios, his success story would have been different. His creativity also helped to unearth the talents of different people who have been behind the successful creation of different animation contents. His vision has helped to steer the company and despite his demise, his legacy stands out making him an inspirational leader to many people today.

Why am I Paying So Much

Warby Parker is a great example of disruptive thinking, research, patience and controlled risk. Warby Parker, and its four founding partners, transformed an industry. Hopefully it serves as an example to other startups and even Fortune 1000 companies on how you build a business that scales as profitable and does good in the world, but doesn't charge a premium. While students at the Warton School of Business, the partners could never understand why eye glasses cost as much as an iPhone. Afterall, there're no rare earth metals in it. It just didn't make sense to them. Typically, when you buy a pair of glasses, you might buy a pair of Ray Bans, Oakley's or Oliver Peoples. Maybe you buy a fashion brand that's licensed like DKNY, Prada, or Channel products. Maybe you go to one of the big chains like Lens Crafters or Pearle Vision, and maybe you pay with your vision insurance like EyeMed. EyeMed, is the second largest vision insurance plan in the country, but what most people don't realize is that this entire ecosystem is owned by one company. That company is Luxottica. Luxottica is a publicly traded company on the New York and Milan exchanges and has a market cap of almost $30 billion. When the Warby Parker founders learned this about the industry, it made sense to them on why customer experiences weren't awesome. Prices for glasses had been rising considerably over the last 20 years or so. It got them even more excited about their model. Usually when you see an 800-pound gorilla, you get terrified. But for them it was an opportunity because they were going to design their own collections, sell direct to consumers online, and by doing so were shortening the value chain. They weren't going to wholesale their product to another company that in turn was going to retail it and mark it up three to five times. So, they had this idea. They loved eyeglasses, but they thought eyeglasses were too expensive, and what if they could sell them directly to consumers online? So, how did they go about doing that? They started Warby Parker with $120,000. They were currently at graduate school foregoing a salary and were working out of their apartments. When starting this business, they wanted to invest as little time and money into this idea as possible before they got the confidence to continue to invest more. That may sound counterintuitive because everyone's always saying take risks, take risks, but they didn't believe that. They were given good advice. If at times you find yourself needing to make a giant leap of faith, they said to step back and break down that decision into a bunch of smaller decisions. So, for them, they had done a lot of customer research. They had surveyed their friends, watched how people buy glasses, and asked people if they would ever buy glasses online? And most people said no. There were enough people that said yes that they did have the competence to continue to move forward. The idea was, what were the three things that they needed to do to truly test this idea? It was to design and build their collection. So, their first collection had 27 shapes, and, two to four colors each. They had to build a website and figure out what was going to be the price that would make the project work?

They initially thought that they could charge $45 for a $500 product. They went to their marketing professor, who was a pricing expert and head of the marketing department at Wharton. They had built this beautiful Power Point business plan and visited his office. They put the business plan on the table and they said, they were going to transform the optical industry by charging $45 for a $500 pair of glasses. And he looked at them and he slid the Power Point presentation back at them. He said, "it wasn't going to work. One tenth the price is outside of the realm of believability. People won't trust your product to be good quality because price is the number one indicator of quality for most people. He said, even if you could pull it off, you're going to have no margin to run your business with, or to market with. No one's going to know you exist because your costs of goods are going to be more expensive than you think it is." Sure enough, the professor was right. As they were building their connection they had opted for better quality components, whether it was five-barrel hinges with Teflon coated screws or custom handmade acetate. Each of those changes in materials increased costs. When they launched their cost of goods it was twice what they thought it was going to be. They put together a survey and they had a product page with a beautiful pair of glasses and they created a bunch of different examples of this survey with different price points from $45 on up. They had randomized samples. They sent the survey out and asked people how likely they are to purchase these pair of glasses? They found that the willingness to purchase increased with the price up until about $100, at which point it plateaued and came down. It seems like $100 is a psychological barrier, so they thought of pricing the glasses at $99. They then thought $99 sounded cheap. $99 sounded like discounting and even though they were going to be providing a fair, accessible price, they want to be an aspirational and inspirational brand. So, they settled on $95. They thought that that sounded deliberate. It visually looked better than $99. And again, the proper impression that they wanted to give.

The other feedback that they got from customers constantly was that they want to touch and feel the glasses. They want to put them on their face. How were they going to do that if they were building a technology company? So, they thought there's got to be a technological solution here. So, they found software where you can upload a photo and virtually try on glasses. The software was okay, but it wasn't great. They kept going back to the drawing board to see what they could do. Finally, they had an "aha" moment where they came up with the idea where you could select five frames. Warby Parker would ship it to them free of cost and they would have five days to try it on at home. That gave them the confidence to keep moving forward, invest more time and money into Warby Parker. Their hope was that this home try on program would also reduce return rates, which would help make ensure that their business was viable.

Then the question was, how do they launch a business like that? For them, they wanted to build a business that they were excited to come to work every day, where they weren't going to roll over and hit the snooze button. That came down to having a positive impact and having a positive impact means any number of things. For them, it meant doing good. To do good, you must be considerate, and they must consider all the different stakeholders that they were impacting, whether it's their customer, so having fair pricing or policies like free shipping and free returns and treating people with dignity. For their employees, it was creating an opportunity to create and grow. Also, having an open office lay out and having 360 reviews on a regular basis and having a deep culture of feedback. That way people did feel like they're learning and growing because the two reasons why people leave their jobs is either because they don't feel like they're learning or because their boss is a jerk. So, if they could create an environment where the bosses were actively mentoring they could create a thriving innovative company for the future.

How do they think about the environment? They believe every company has negative environmental impacts, but the best ones can track those and figuring out ways to minimize them, and at times negate them completely. So, they track their carbon emissions from the production of their frames and their factories, to the edging of their lenses and their optical labs, to shipping from their warehouses to their customers, to the electricity used in their offices, to their stores. They introduced a sustainability scorecard, so they can figure out how they can reduce the impact of the construction as they build out their new stores.

Then the question was how to impact the community and that was the fourth stakeholder. For Warby Parker, even bringing down the price of the glasses in the US to $95, there were still 700 million people around the world that don't have access to glasses. They thought that that was unforgivable. Reading glasses were invented 800 years ago. As humanity, they thought, they were failing. So, they asked themselves if there was a market-based solution. Prior to going to business school, Neil Blumenthal spent five years working at a nonprofit called Vision Spring, that trained low income women to start their own businesses, giving eye exams and selling glasses to people in their communities. This was a great model because it created jobs, it created the economic incentive for people to distribute glasses in their communities on an ongoing basis, but it also treated people with dignity because, you can imagine, that even if you're living on less than $4 a day, you don't want to be wearing a pair of donated 1970's cat eyes. They look ridiculous and those same social norms that are here in the states are the same in rural

Bangladesh. So, by selling glasses in these communities, through a nonprofit manner the prices are subsidized to make sure that they are affordable. So, in places like Indian Bangladesh they might be $2 to $4 and in places like Guatemala, El Salvador, it might be $6 to $8. You treat somebody as a value conscious consumer rather than a needy beneficiary and you design according to their needs and wants. You have the same empathy as you would if you were building a business selling glasses here in the US. So, for every pair of glasses they sell, they distribute one to someone in need through this nonprofit Vision Spring. Every month they tally up the number of glasses sold, and they make a cash donation to Vision Spring to allow them to procure that number of glasses and in turn sell those to entrepreneurs that they've trained across the developing world who in turn sell it in their communities.

Today, Warby Parker is one of the fastest growing and most successful firm's today because of the disruptive thinking, research, patience, and customer centric philosophy. In the end, Warby Parker, their customers, and the eyewear community are all winners.

CREATIVE EXERCISE

"I can't understand why people are frightened of new ideas. I'm frightened of the old ones."
John Cage, composer

WHAT IS ANOTHER MEANING FOR THAT SIGN?

For most of us, we have taken a written road test to get our driver's license. One of the things we needed to learn was the meaning of street signs. Many street signs are just illustrations with no words. It could be swerves in the road, no parking, intersection, do not enter, etc.

Your exercise is to think about other meanings that street signs may have. When you see a street sign ask yourself, "what are alternative meanings to that traffic sign? **Warning...don't forget to keep your eyes on the road.!**

"You can't keep bitch-slapping your creativity, or it will run away and find a new pimp."
George Meyer, producer and writer

COMMUNICATE...OLD SCHOOL!

In today's age of technology, we have numerous ways to communicate. Think about how you communicate to your clients and colleagues. You have telephone, intercom, email, internet, intranet, social media, etc. What would happen if you needed to communicate with clients and colleagues but the power went out for days? Let's go a step further. What if you couldn't leave your desk? You are confined to your desk and have no electricity.

Your exercise is to imagine living in this scenario. How would you build a communication system for you and your office? How would you communicate back and forth with your teammates? I know the obvious answer would be to yell, but eventually you would lose your voice. **Go forth and communicate.**

"The best way to have a good idea is to have lots of ideas."
Linus Pauling

COFFEE IS NOT COFFEE...IT IS A TOMATO

Our minds are trained to recognize objects and give them a name. We see a desk and we recognize and call it a desk. We see a telephone and we recognize and call it a telephone. Look around you and name all the objects you can see.

Your exercise is to look at all those objects and give them new names. You now recognize and rename that desk as a giraffe. The phone may now be an orchid. How many objects can you rename before you run out of names? Every day for a week play this game. You should see the number of renamed objects increase daily. Instead of waking up and getting a cup of coffee out of the coffee pot, wake up and get a box of tomato out of the tomato screen. **Enjoy the tomato.**

"Follow the path of the unsafe, independent thinker. Expose your ideas to the dangers of controversy. Speak your mind and fear less the label of 'crackpot' than the stigma of conformity. And on issues that seem important to you, stand up and be counted at any cost."
Thomas J. Watson, past CEO of IBM

YOUR NAME IS A PICASSO

A letter or number is more than a letter or a number. It is a creative form. Some could say they are artistic forms. Look at the letters and numbers differently. Flip them around. Turn them inside out. Change their shape and form. Turn them into artistic forms.

Your exercise is to take your full name and turn it into an artistic form. Flip the letters around, change the fonts, change the style, and change the colors. Turn your name into a piece of art. How beautiful can you make your name? **Create your own Picasso.**

"A simple idea can, inspire, motivate, and produce change."

"A good traveler is one who knows how to travel with their mind."
Michael Bassey Johnson, poet, playwright and novelist

YOU MAY BE THE NEXT ARMANI

Your desk is your desk. You were probably assigned or given your desk. Perhaps you picked out your own desk. Regardless, take a good look at your desk. How functional is it? Is the space, shape and size optimal? How are the power sources? Is it attractive? Is it comfortable?

Your exercise is to design your own desk/work space. Don't design it in your mind…put it on paper. Design it like you are a Desk Engineer. Be creative and functional. Draw it up so a manufacturer could understand the drawing well enough to build it. **You could become the next Armani of office furniture.**

"Ideas are the factors that lift civilization. They create revolutions. There is more dynamite in an idea than in many bombs."
Bishop Vincent

"The true sign of intelligence is not knowledge but imagination."
Albert Einstein

SHOULD SATURDAY REALLY BE SATURDAY?

Back in 400 AD in Rome, the Romans adopted the seven days in a week idea. It eventually spread to Europe and then the rest of the world. The name of each day was related to Roman mythology. It is over 1600 years since the adoption of those names. The world has changed so it is time to rename the days to fit our times.

Your exercise is to rename the days of the week. They can have a theme or be loosely connected. The names can be any size and can mean anything. Perhaps you invent new words and names. The only requirement is that each day ends with the suffix "-day." **Be the person that changes the calendar for the next 1600 years.**

"Great minds discuss ideas. Average minds discuss events. Small minds discuss people."
Henry Thomas Buckle

WHO'S YOUR LEAGUE?

Professional sports leagues usually have logos that are two or three colors with a silhouette of a player or ball with negative space.

Your exercise is to design your own logo for a sports league participating in these activities:

Pizza Eating

Wind Surfing

Gardening

Grocery Shopping

Internet Surfing

What's your logo?

"Imagination is more important than knowledge."
Albert Einstein

EXTRAORDINARY OR "OUT-OF-THE-ORDINARY?"

I have always said "the most successful people in business are either extraordinary or out-of-the-ordinary." What I mean by extraordinary people are people who are better at a particular aspect of the something. If your industry is focusing on service, there is usually someone or some firm that is better than the rest at it. These people and firms are extraordinary and everyone is chasing them. The other very successful person or firm looks at what everyone else is doing and finds a different road to travel. They do the "out-of-the-ordinary." Think about the airline industry many years ago. All the airlines were concentrating their efforts on improving their services. They were offering more and more. They were all trying to "keep up with the Joneses." Southwest Airlines did the "out-of-the-ordinary." They went the opposite way and cut out the frills and offered cheap fares. That differentiation made them very successful. Now, the airline industry keeps a keen eye on Southwest and what they will come up with next. Sometimes, just doing the opposite is all you need to do to find success. Instead of adding services, cut out the frills and lower the price. That might be what the consumers crave.

Your exercise is to write down five things that everyone in your industry does, the things that every firm is focused on improving, and then do the opposite. If you did the opposite, how could that help you? Write down the pros of doing the opposite. Are you on to anything? **Opposites can attract.**

"You can never solve a problem on the level on which it was created."
Albert Einstein

BRING BACK THAT IDEA

Thomas Edison once said, "Many of life's failures are people who did not realize how close they were to success when they gave up."

Your exercise is to list five ideas in your life that you gave up on.

Bring them back to life and see where they might take you. **Bring those ideas back to life.**

"Creativity involves breaking out of established patterns
in order to look at things in a different way."
Edward de Bono

IT AIN'T AS SIMPLE AS YOU THINK

Sometimes we take for granted some of the simplest things. There are things that we do every day that we take for granted. Have you ever thought about how you tie the laces to your shoes or button your shirt?

Your exercise is to write detailed instructions on how you tie the laces of your shoes. **Don't get yourself knotted up.**

"The difficulty lies not so much in developing new ideas as escaping from old ones."
John Maynard Keynes

WHERE IS X?

Do you know where everything is in your office or work space? Do you know where every letter is in your space? I'm not talking about letters that you send or received in the mail or electronically. I'm talking about the alphabet.

Your exercise is to use your cell phone or camera to take a picture of every letter in the alphabet that you can find in your work space.

No two letters can come from the same object. **Warning... "X" isn't easy to find.**

"Creativity can solve almost any problem. The creative art, the defeat of habit by originality, overcomes everything."
George Lois, art director, designer and author

THAT WAS MY IDEA

Have you ever had an idea and someone else had the same idea, but they followed through on it and made a lot of money? The answer is probably yes. I call these "Million Dollar Ideas" that got away from me. There are two important things to learn here. Produce as many "Million Dollar Ideas" as you can and act on those "Million Dollar Ideas."

Your exercise is to put together a running list of all your "Million Dollar Ideas." Also go around to all you colleagues and friends and ask them to add to your list. If you and your pals know that an idea that can make you grossly rich is one idea away, your mind will create numerous ideas. **Get grossly rich.**

"It's easy to attack and destroy an act of creation.
It's a lot more difficult to perform one."
Chuck Palahniuk, novelist

BURST THE BARRIER!

Fear of being wrong will prevent you from achieving greatness. Many people put up barriers to protect themselves from being wrong. Most of the people do this. If you want to achieve greatness you need to get past these mental and physical barriers. Every day we see physical barriers to prevent things from happening outside those barriers. We also have mental barriers that prevent us from stepping out of our comfort zone to create something new and different. We need to get past those physical and mental barriers.

Your exercise is to take pictures of physical barriers around you that prohibit "something" from happening. This could be an executive assistant, acting as the gatekeeper to the president of your firm. Wouldn't the President like to hear your great idea? Also write down mental barriers that prevent you from exploring new ideas. Take 10 physical or mental pictures and think about why they protect or prohibit you. Once you know if that barrier protects or prohibits you, then you will be ready to burst through those barriers.

Nothing should get in your way to greatness.

"I never made one of my discoveries through
the process of rational thinking"
Albert Einstein

LET THE GAMES BEGIN

If you are like me and many others, you grew up loving sports. As a youth I would play sports whenever I could. I would still love to live that lifestyle, but this thing called a job gets in the way. Now, I only have time to play after work. How could I change that so I could play at work?

Your exercise is to invent a sport that you can play at your desk with objects that you have in your area. Dream up the game and write the rules and regulations of your new sport. Maybe it will be an Olympic event someday. **Let the games begin.**

"Imagination is everything. It is the preview of life's attractions."
Albert Einstein

I HEAR YOU

I love James Bond movies. One of my favorite parts of these movies is when they roll out the new gadgets. What are your favorite 007 gadgets? Weather it is a jetpack in "Thunderball," a portable gyrocopter in "You Only Live Twice," or the laser piston gun in "Golden Eye," he is always equipped with cool devices. It would be awesome if we could have his cool gadgets.

Your exercise is to design your own gadget designed to spy on your competitions board meetings. What would the gadget look like, what would it be able to do? How do you control it? Just think how much we could learn about our competition if we had this Spy gadget. Design it and draw it up. **There are no secrets.**

"All achievements, all earned riches, have their beginning in an idea."
Napoleon

"I like to listen. I have learned a great deal from listening carefully. Most people never listen."
Ernest Hemmingway

I ALWAYS DO THAT

Over the years, we have become creatures of habit. We have developed routines. Why have we developed these routines? Many professionals would say it is for safety. If we do the same thing every day, there is the safety of knowing the outcome. Think about your routines. You wake up for work at the same time. You have a very structured routine to get dressed and get out of your house to go to work. You take the same route to work. You get your cup of coffee at the same place. You get to work at the same time. You get the idea. We are creatures of routines. The problem is routines stifle creativity.

Your exercise is to write down 15 things, routines, you do every day. Think about why you do each one of them. Now, think about how you can break those routines. Now do it! Take a different route to and from work. Get your coffee from somewhere else, etc. Open your mind to different ideas. **Don't get stifled by routines.**

"Creativity takes courage."

"The only constant in our business is that everything is changing. We have to take advantage of change and not let it take advantage of us. We have to be ahead of the game."
Michael Dell

WHAT IS IN THE LOGO?

A logo should be designed to identify with the brand. Some are very successful, most are not. A logo should allow the user to have an idea of what business they are in just by their logo. Can you identify logos that are identifiable to a business?

Your exercise is to have a friend or colleague cut out logos from magazines. Make sure the logo doesn't have the company name on it. Also, have them write the name of the company and their industry on the back of the logo. I want you to do two things. First, without reading the back of the logo, can you identify the business they are in? Two, take the logos that you cannot identify with and read what industry they are in. Redesign their logo to be more identifiable with their industry. **Be a designer.**

"Where all think alike, no one thinks very much."
Walter Lippmann

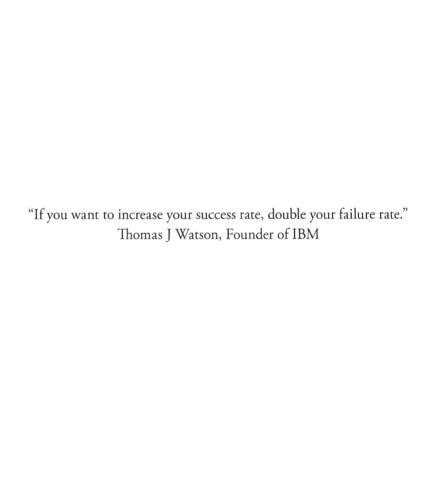

"If you want to increase your success rate, double your failure rate."
Thomas J Watson, Founder of IBM

IT'S JUST A BRICK

I look at rocks differently these days. You may look at a rock as just another object. Usually we are trying to move or remove rocks. They are often getting in our way. They are a nuisance. A few years ago, a guy came up with the silliest idea that made him a fortune. Take a little rock, name it, stick it in a box and call it a "Pet Rock." Are you kidding me? No, I'm not kidding you. One Christmas it was the big seller. Some creative guy took this simple rock and found a different use for it and made a fortune.

Your exercise is to take a brick and think on 50 things you can do with that brick. You will probably start with building a house, wall, walkway and driveway. After that you will get creative. **Maybe you will have the next Pet Rock.**

"An unhatched idea is nothing more than just another idea that dies on the vine."
Michael Balch

HATCH AN IDEA

We often explain new ideas by associating them with old ideas. We think in metaphors. It makes sense; people struggle to understand a completely new concept. The military loves to give metaphoric names to their weapons. Think about the army designing a missile that is capable of seeking out heat from an enemy vehicle and attacking it. Instead of explaining how it works, just give it a name that people can identify with. There is a snake, called a sidewinder that detects the heat of their prey and attacks it. It's no coincidence that the heat seeking missile is called the "Sidewinder." It is no coincidence that the bomb that gets dropped in the mountains of Afghanistan to clear foliage and vegetation, for the purpose of creating landing zones for helicopters, is called a "Daisy Cutter."

Your exercise is to find 10 things in your house or office and develop a metaphor for them. **"Brood" over the exercise and "hatch" a great metaphor.**

"The chief enemy of creativity is good sense."
Pablo Picasso

"You can't use up creativity. The more you use, the more you have."
Maya Angelou, poet, author, dancer, actress and singer

"Creativity requires the courage
to let go of certainties."
Erich Fromm, psychologist and Author

"Creativity is contagious. Pass it on."
Albert Einstein

MISSION IMPOSSIBLE

Our world is ever changing. There are advances being made every day. Technology, for one, is moving and changing at break neck speeds. Think about how all these changes have affected you and your business.

Your exercise is to look around your business, or your home, and think about if you could make the impossible possible. Come up with an invention that would help you. Just a few years ago people would have never thought of driving and walking around talking on the cell phone. The personal computer was a complete game changer. What would you invent that would change your life. With your new invention, how would it affect your life? Would it make it better or make other things more complicated? **Make the impossible possible.**

"Thank goodness I was never sent to school; it would have rubbed off some of the originality."
Beatrix Potter, Author

"Ideas are like rabbits. You get a couple and learn how to handle them, and pretty soon you have a dozen."
John Steinbeck, author

WHERE DID THAT WORD COME FROM?

Have you ever thought about who and how words are invented? Who came up with the word computer, tire, chair, car or apple? If you are a Latin scholar, you can build words using Latin meanings. But, who invented all those Latin words? Think of all the words in the dictionary. Where did they come from and what went into making them words?

Your exercise is to take something you know and change the word. It can be something you use every day or a project that you are working on. You can invent an entirely new word, combine two or more existing words or use your Latin education to describe your new word. **Be a Wordsmith.**

"Imitation is suicide."
Ralph Waldo Emerson

WHERE DO IDEAS COME FROM?

As I wrote earlier in this book, an idea is often taking two known ideas and combining them into on new idea. Did Steve Jobs think a cell phone and a personal computer combined would be a great idea? Probably. I'm sure it wasn't an accident. There are so many things we touch every day that are a combination of two known ideas that combined into a new idea. Think about what they are.

Your exercise is to invent a new product. Can you think of two things, or items, that you know and combine them into one new idea? Start with one new idea. Don't stop there. Keep combining old ideas. Before you know it, you may have the next iPhone. **Be the next Steve Jobs.**

"If we could only pull out our brain and use only our eyes."
Pablo Picasso

"Creativity is the power to connect the seemingly unconnected."
William Plomer, author

BREAK THE STATUS QUO

Humans tend to conform to the status quo. As I stated earlier in this book, humans like routines. The "status quo," routine, is safe and comfortable. How many times do you get annoyed with the status quo and don't do anything about it.

Your exercise is to write down ten things that you do every day that bug you or your clients. After you write the list of ten things that annoy you and/or your clients, try to CREATE a new way to solve the annoyance. This should help make your life and business a little bit better. **Stop being annoyed.**

"Creativity is as important as literacy."
Sir Kenneth Robinson, author, speaker, advisor on education

DON'T FLOP

Many times knowledge gets in our way. Albert Einstein once said, "Imagination is more important than knowledge." We often think that just because we have been doing things the same way for years that it must be the correct way. Prior to 1968, the conventional way to jump over the bar of the high jump in the Olympics was either to dive over head first or hurdle the bar. That was the common thought for over a century. Prior to the 1968 Olympics, a medical student, Dick Fosbury, researched the human body and came up with a thought that the best way to jump over a high bar was not to dive or hurdle, but it was to jump over with his back to the bar. It later became known as the "Fosbury Flop." Not only did the new method win him the gold medal in 1968, but it revolutionized the sport.

Your exercise is to build a presentation on how to ignore existing knowledge. It sounds simple, but it is not. **Lose all existing knowledge.**

"To live a creative life, we must lose our fear of being wrong."
Joseph Chilton Pearce, Author

"Courage is what it takes to stand up and speak;
courage is also what it takes to sit down and listen.
Winston Churchill

FIND THAT NEEDLE

A good idea isn't always the best idea. When people sit around and try to solve a problem, or find a solution, they often accept the first good idea. Great problem solvers and creative people don't stop with the first answer. They push on to see if they can find a better solution. Truly successful people never stop trying to improve on ideas. Albert Einstein was asked, "What is the difference between you and the rest of us?" He replied, "If you are asked to look for a needle in a haystack, then you search until you find it, whereas I search until I find all the needles."

Your exercise is to push to find a better solution. The next time you're in a meeting with people and trying to find a solution, be the person that doesn't automatically agree with a good solution. See if you can make that solution better. People will probably get annoyed with you, but they will learn to respect a better solution. **Look for all the needles in the haystack.**

"Creativity arises from our ability to see things from many different angles."
Keri Smith, Author

"Only those who will risk going too far can possibly find out how far one can go."
T.S. Elliot

DOES AN IDEA STAND A CHANCE?

In today's day and age, it is so difficult to get an idea through. So often an idea gets criticized or ridiculed in front of your peers. This thwarts the chances of presenting another idea. This has been going on since the beginning of time. Every day, people's creative ideas are getting shut down without them ever having a chance. How many great ideas never surfaced? How different would our world today be if creative ideas were openly accepted?

Your exercise is not to give in. The next time you have an idea, run it up the flagpole. If, it gets shot down, and it probably will, don't get down and discouraged. Instead, fight for your idea. Be heard. Push them on your idea. This is typically not a comfortable thing to do. What is the worst thing they can do to you, put you in front of a firing squad? **Stand up for your idea.**

"Courage is being scared to death… and saddle up anyway."
John Wayne

FIND THE JUICE

Denise Shekerjian, author of <u>Uncommon Genius</u>, wrote "Staying loose, allowing yourself the freedom to ramble, opening yourself up to outside influences, keeping a flexible mind willing to entertain all sorts of notions and avenues – this is the attitude that is most appropriate for the start of any project where the aim is to generate something new." There are many books and articles written on how to create an idea. Many of them give you a list of things you need to do to generate an idea. It is my opinion that it is very difficult to force ideas. A good creative mind generates lots of ideas. Ideas come from different places. The more open your mind is the more freely ideas will pour out. If you have checklists and a structure to generating ideas, your mind will be focusing on the checklists and not on the freedom of thinking freely and unconstrained. The bottom line is that you need to free your mind of organized thinking to let the creativity out.

Your exercise is to do creative projects that you rarely or have never done in the past. Get paper and crayons and draw anything. Don't learn how to draw, just draw. Write some poetry. Hum a new song. Free you mind. Stir up your creative juices. If you do that you will be amazed how ideas will start flowing. **Start stirring the juices.**

"To live a creative life we most first lose the fear of being wrong."
Joseph Chilton Pearce, author

WHAT'S YOUR FIRST THOUGHT?

People often say, "Your first thought (or idea) is your best thought." That can be true, but it also could be a very common idea. There is a word called "ideamation." "Ideamation" is defined as the first idea that everyone thinks of. If solving your problem is obvious to others, there is a good chance they will have similar solutions. If you are trying to differentiate yourself, "ideamation" can be a bad thing. If you think you have and great idea, ask yourself, "is the idea obvious to others?" If the answer is yes, come up with another idea.

Your exercise is to take a problem that you are trying to solve to a few of you colleagues and ask them what their solution would be to the problem. If any of them have the same solution as you, go back to the drawing board and find a new solution to the problem. Your first idea may not be your best idea. **Dig deep and find multiple ideas.**

"The only constant in our business is that everything is changing. We have to take advantage of change and not let it take advantage of us. We have to be ahead of the game."
Michael Dell

SELL IT!

Advertising executive, David M. Ogilvy, once said, "In the modern world of business, it is useless to be a creative thinker unless you can sell what you create. Management cannot be expected to recognize a good idea unless it is presented to them by a good salesman." How true this is. I have been in the financial service business for many, many years. When I first started on Wall Street in NYC my mentor told me, "The best Research Analyst is the one who is the best salesman." Many years later that theory still holds true. A good idea isn't anything unless it is sold well.

Your exercise is to take one of the many ideas that you have written down in this book and sell it. Work on your presentation. If this is something that you are not comfortable doing, find a friend or a colleague that you think is a good sales person. Ask for their help to build yourself a sales pitch. Work on your pitch, then get a group of your friends, peers, or management team and sell them on your idea. **Become a salesperson.**

"Every act of creation is first an act of destruction."
Pablo Picasso

GO BACK TO SCHOOL

I wrote in the first chapter of this book about how traditional schooling has thwarted CREATIVITY. Remember when we were in school drawing and our teachers were critical that we were drawing outside the lines? Now, I chuckle every time I hear someone criticize how people can't think outside-outside-box.

Your exercise is to take a half day off from what you are doing and go back to kindergarten. Yes…go back to kindergarten. Offer to help out for a couple of hours. Think of a problem you are trying to solve. While thinking of a solution to the problem and sitting among the kids, who naturally think outside-the-box, you will probably start to think differently. Believe it or not (think positively) those kindergarteners' views will rub off on you and hopefully you will have a new solution to your problem. **Go back to the future.**

"A question that sometimes drives me hazy: am I or the others crazy?"
Albert Einstein

WHAT IS IN THAT SAYING?

We often use metaphors and proverbs to describe things. How many times have you ever heard that "the grass is greener on the other side" which means things are better at some other place? How about "curiosity killed the cat?" That poor cat is dead because it was curious? I can't believe some animal loving group has not tried to eradicate that saying from our society. Think if you were to change the proverb or metaphor. Things would be different if "curiosity fed the cat," or "the grass is greener on the other side." Just by changing or taking out one word, in each proverb completely changed the meaning of that proverb.

Your exercise is to think about a metaphor or proverb that you use in your business today and change it around to change its meaning. Then think about how that new metaphor or proverb can be used to help your business. **Change the direction of that saying and turn your business around.**

"Every fool can see what is wrong. See what is good in it!"
Winston Churchill

POSITIVE THINKING

Composer John Cage once said, "I can't understand why people are frightened of new ideas. I'm frightened of the old ones."

Your exercise over the next week is to list every new idea you hear. Don't dismiss any. Write down three reasons why each idea is a good idea. Don't write down any reasons why it is not a good idea. This will open your mind to positive thinking. Positive thinking results in positive things. **Negative thinking results in negative things.**

"To improve is to change; to be perfect is to change often."
Winston Churchill

RETAKE THAT TEST

Albert Einstein was once asked by his students, "This is the same test as you gave us before." Einstein replied, "The same questions, but the answers are different."

Your exercise is to rewrite your business plan and chart a different course. If you don't have a fresh business plan then write two plans taking different paths. There is more than one path. **What is the best path?**

"Children enter school as question marks and leave as periods."
Neil Postman, author

THROUGH A KID'S EYES

So often we get comfortable with what we know. We forget what we didn't know. When we first start a new job we look around at our new surrounding with all sorts of questions and ideas. After a period of time, we fall in line with the party line. Think about how curious a child is. The opportunities are unlimited for them. They are often looking at things for the first time. They see things differently. That is how we felt when we were curious kids. It would be great to look at things in our business with no preconceived notions of how things are expected to be. It would be great to look at our business through a kid's eyes.

Your exercise is to look at your business through fresh eyes. Ask a friend, or a college student to visit your business. Explain to them what you are trying to accomplish, but don't tell them how you do it. Ask them how they would do it? They will give you that fresh view of your business. **See your business through a kid's eyes.**

"Creativity can solve almost any problem. The creative act, the defeat of habit by originality, overcomes everything."
George Lois, creativity author

WHERE DO I FIND IDEAS?

Where do you think the best? You will often read or hear from creative thinkers that the four B's are where many people do their best thinking. What are the four B's? They are:

Bars
Bathrooms
Buses
Beds

The other obvious ones that don't start with B are running, working out, waiting for the kids, carpooling, fishing, watching TV, work, etc. We all have places where we are more creative.

Your exercise is to identify where you come up with your best ideas. Once you have your places of creativity, spend more time there. I'm not saying to spend the entire work day in the shower, but I would suggest longer showers. I'm not suggesting you spend the work day running, but I would suggest running more or longer.

Let's hit the shower.

People who have stopped thinking do what they have always done. DON'T STOP THINKING!

WHAT IS IN THE FUTURE?

I often say, "The greatest accomplishments in history have yet to be achieved." There will always be a greater play, song, painting, etc. Records will be broken. Things will be invented. The world as we know it is always evolving. Think about your life. How has it evolved since your birth? How will it evolve going forward?

Your exercise is to think about your business today. What will it look like 1, 3, 5, 10, 50 and 100 hundred years from now? Don't worry about being wrong. Who will be around in 100 years to tell you that you were wrong? Set out with what you know today and dream about what the future could look like. **Dream big or go home.**

"The most powerful factors in the world are clear ideas
in the minds of energetic men of good will."
J. Arthur Thomson, author

THE CENTURY OF IDEAS

Seth Godin, who is a marketing expert and author, once said "the first 100 years of our country's history were about who could build the biggest, most efficient farm. And the second century focused on the race to build factories. Welcome to the third century, folks. The third century is about ideas."

Your exercise is to go to Seth Godin's blog and sign up. This blog is full of ideas and motivation. He gets your CREATIVITY juices flowing. **Squeeze those juices out.**

"The social consequences of releasing creative
abilities are potentially enormous."
J.P. Guilford, researcher of creativity

LIST YOUR OFFICE

Have you ever noticed how positive all real estate listings are? If the rooms are small, they call them charming. If there is a large room, it is spacious. A nice patio is an outdoor living area. They accent the positive and they deemphasize the faults.

Your exercise is to build a real estate listing for your work area. If you have an office, describe your office and neighboring offices. If you are in a cubicle, accent the positives of the space and deemphasize the negatives. **Sell your cubicle!**

REFERENCES

Baker, J. H. (2006). *Sisters: The Lives of America's Suffragists*. New York, NY: Hill and Wang.

Berg, J. M. (2016). Balancing on the creative high-wire: Forecasting the success of novel ideas in organizations. Retrieved from http://justinmberg.com/berg_2016_asq_creative.pdf

Bertoni, M. & Brunello, G. (2013, October 26). Laterborns don't give up: The effects of birth order on earnings in Europe. *IZA Discussion Paper No. 7679*. Retrieved from https://www.econstor.eu/bitstream/10419/90106/1/dp7679.pdf

Bolton, L. E. (2006). Believing in First Mover Advantage. Retrieved from http://citeseerx.ist.psu.edu/viewdoc/download?doi=10.1.1.725.3691&rep=rep1&type=pdf

Blumenthal, Neil (2016) How Neil Blumenthal's Eye Doctor Inspired Him to Start Warby Parker https://www.inc.com/video/how-warby-parker-started-with-one-very-big-idea.html

Bronson, Po, and Ashley Merryman. "The creativity crisis." (2010): 44-49.

Brown, Joel. "Reason Why You Have Lost Your Creativity." 7 Dec 2017.

Dane, E. (2010). Reconsidering the trade-off between enterprise and flexibility: A cognitive entrenchment perspective. *Academy of Management Review, 35*(4): 579-603.

Dane, E., Rockmann, K. W., & Pratt, M. G. (2012). When should I trust my gut? Linking domain expertise to intuitive decision-making effectiveness. *Organizational Behavior and Human Decision Processes, 119*(2): 187-194.

Della Cava, M. (2014, October 15). Linda Rottenberg's tips for crazy entrepreneurs. *USA Today.* Retrieved from https://www.usatoday.com/story/tech/2014/10/02/linda-rottenberg-crazy-is-a-compliment-book/16551377/

Falkner, D. (1995). *Great Time Coming: The Life of Jackie Robinson, from Baseball to Birmingham.* New York, NY: Simon & Schuster.

Fragale, A. R., Overbeck, J. R., & Neale, M. A. (2011). Resources versus respect: Social judgments based on targets' power and status positions. *Journal f experimental social psychology, 47*(4): 767-775.

Galenson, D. (2011). *Old Masters and Young Geniuses: The Two Life Cycles of Artistic Creativity.* Princeton, NJ: Princeton University Press.

Godart, F. C., Maddux, W. W., Shipilov, A. V., & Galinsky, A. D. (2015). Fashion with a foreign flair: Professional experiences abroad facilitate the creative innovations of organizations. *Academy of Management Journal, 58*(1): 195-220.

Golder, P. N. & Tellis, G. J. (1993). Pioneer advantage: Marketing logic or marketing legend? *Journal of Marketing Research, 30*(): 158-170.

Grant A. & Sandberg, S. (foreword) (2017). *Originals: How Non-Conformists Move the World.* New York, NY: Penguin Books.

Hansen, D. (2005). *The Dream: Martin Luther King, Jr., and the Speech that Inspired a Nation.* New York, NY: Harper Perennial.

Hirschman, A. O. (1970). *Exit, Voice, and Loyalty: Responses to Decline in Firms, Organizations, and States.* Cambridge, MA: Harvard University Press.

Hitt, J. (2013, Aug. 17). An inventor wants one less wire to worry about. *New York Times*. Retrieved from https://www.nytimes.com/2013/08/18/technology/an-inventor-wants-one-less-wire-to-worry-about.html

Jick, T. D. & Gentile, M. (1995, Dec. 11). Donna Dubinsky and Apple Computer, Inc. (A). *Harvard Business School*, Case 9-486-083.

Jones, C. B. (2011), *Behind the Dream: The Making of the Speech that Transformed a Nation*. New York, NY: Palgrave Macmillan.

Jost, J. T., Pelham, B. W., Sheldon, O., & Ni Sullivan, B. (2003). Social inequality and the reduction of ideological dissonance on behalf of the system: Evidence of enhanced system justification among the disadvantaged. *European Journal of Psychology, 33*(1): 13-36.

Jung, W., King, B. G., & Soule, S. A. (2014). Issue bricolage: Explaining the configuration of the social movement sector, 1960-1995. *American Journal of Sociology, 120*(1): 187-225.

Kafka, P. (2015, Dec. 1). First came nerve. Then came Babble. Rufus Griscom's third act: A buzzfeed for brains. *Recode*. Retrieved from https://www.recode.net/2015/12/1/11621034/first-came-nerve-then-came-babble-rufus-griscoms-third-act-a-buzzfeed

Kelly, L. & Medina, C. (2014). *Rebels at Work: A Handbook for Leading Change from Within*. New York, NY: O'Reilly Media.

Kerr, A. M. (1992). *Lucy Stone: Speaking Out for Equality*. Rutgers, NJ: Rutgers University Press.

King, Jr., M. L. (1998). *The Autobiography of Martin Luther King Jr.* New York, NY: Warner Books.

Kotter, J. P. (1996). *Leading Change*. Boston: Harvard Business School Press.

Kozbelt, A. (2007). A quantitative analysis of Beethoven as self-critic: Implications for psychological theories of musical creativity. *Psychology of music, 35*(1): 144-168.

Mackinnon, D. W. (1962). The nature and nurture of creative talent. *American Psychologist, 17*(7): 484-495.

March, J. (1994). *A Primer on Decision-Making: How Decisions Happen.* New York, NY: Free Press.

Marshall, Andrew C. (2013) There's a critical difference between creativity and innovation. *Business Insider.*

Retrieved from https://www.businessinsider.com/difference-between-creativity-and-innovation-2013-4

Mellor, L. (2014, November 7). Seinfeld's journey from flop to acclaimed hit. *Den of Geek.* Retrieved from http://www.denofgeek.com/dvd-bluray/seinfeld/32857/seinfeld-s-journey-from-flop-to-acclaimed-hit

Meyerson, D. E. & Scully, M. A. (1995). Tempered radicalism and the politics of ambivalence and change. *Organization Science, 6*(5): 585-600.

Nadkarni, S. & Herman, Pol. (2010). CEO personality, strategic flexibility, and firm performance: The case of Indian Business Process Outsourcing Industry. *Academy of Management Journal, 53*(5): 1050-1073.

Oliner, P. S. & Oliner, P. (1992). *The Altruistic Personality: Rescuers of Jews in Nazi Europe.* New York, NY: Touchstone.

PandoDaily (2013, May 24). *John Doerr on what went wrong with the Segway* [Video file]. Retrieved from https://www.youtube.com/watch?v=oOQzjpBkUTY

Pannapacker, W. A. (2009, February 20). How to procrastinate like Leonardo da Vinci. *Chronicle Review.*

Pontikes, E. G. & Barnett, W. P. (2014). When to be a nonconformist entrepreneur? Organizational responses to vital events. *University of Chicago Working Paper No. 12-59.*

Raffiee, J. & Feng, J. (2014). Should I quit my day job? A hybrid path to entrepreneurship. *Academy of Management Journal, 37*(4): 936-963.

Root-Bernstein, R., Allen, L., Beach, L., Bhadula, R., Fast, J., Hosey, C. ...& Weinlander, S. (2008). Arts foster scientific success:

Avocations of Nobel, National Academy, Royal Society, and Sigma XI Members. *Journal of Psychology of Science and Technology, 1*(2): 51-63.

Schumpeter, J. A. (2008). *Capitalism, Socialism, & Democracy* (3rd Ed.). New York, NY: Harper Perennial Modern Classics.

Shin, J. (2015). Putting work off pays off: The hidden benefits of procrastination for creativity (Manuscript under review).

Simonton, D. K. (2011). Creativity and discovery as blind variation: Campbell's (1960) BVSR model after the half-century mark. *Review of General Psychology, 15*(): 158-174.

Simonton, D. K. (Ed.) (2014). *The Wiley Handbook of Genius.* Hoboken, NJ: Wiley-Blackwell.

Smith, R. (2009). *The Leap: How 3 Simple Changes Can Propel Your Career from Good to Great.* New York, NY: Penguin.

Sulloway, F. J. & Zweigenhaft, R. L. (2010). Birth order and risk-taking in athletics: A meta-analysis and study of major league baseball. *Personality and Social Psychology Review, 14*(4): 402-416.

Sulloway, F. J. (1997). *Born to Rebel: Birth Order, Family Dynamics, and Creative Lives.* New York, NY: Vintage.

Sulloway, F. J. (2010). Why siblings are like Darwin's Finches: Birth order, sibling competition, and adaptive divergence within the family. In D. M. Buss & P. H. Hawley (Eds.), *The Evolution of Personality and Individual Differences* (pp. 86-119). New York, NY: Oxford University Press.

Team YS & Khera, S. (2017, June 20). Timing–Crucial factor behind failure and success of startups. *YOURSTORY.* Retrieved from https://yourstory.com/2017/06/timing-crucial-factor-for-startups/

Thayer, K. (2016, July 1). How the co-CEOs of Warby Parker set their sights on success and impact. *Forbes.* Retrieved from https://www.forbes.com/sites/katherynthayer/2016/07/01/how-the-co-ceos-of-warby-parker-set-their-sights-on-success-and-impact/

The Economist (2013, April 13). How might your choice of browser affect your job prospects? *The Economist*. Retrieved from https://www.economist.com/the-economist-explains/2013/04/10/how-might-your-choice-of-browser-affect-your-job-prospects

White, J. B. & Langer, E. L. (1999). Horizontal hostility: Relations between similar minority groups. *Journal of Social Issues, 55*(3): 537-559.

Chao, R.O., Lopez-Gottardi, C. "How America's Education Model Kills Creativity and Entrepreneurship." *Forbes* 3 Oct 2015.

Creemers, Bert PM, and Gerry J. Reezigt. "The concept of vision in educational effectiveness theory and research." *Learning Environments Research 2.2* (1999): 107-135.

ECOTEC. "External evaluation of the European Year of Creativity." 2009.

Gabora, Liane, and Scott Barry Kaufman. "Evolutionary approaches to creativity." *The Cambridge handbook of creativity* (2010): 279-300.

Gray, Peter. "As Children's Freedom Has Declined, So Has Their Creativity." *Psychology Today* 17 Sep 2012. <https://www.psychologytoday.com/us/blog/freedom-learn/201209/children-s-freedom-has-declined-so-has-their-creativity>.

Kim, KH. "The Creativity Crisis In America!" *THECREATIVITY* 10 Jul 2012.

Kim, Kyung Hee. "The creativity crisis: The decrease in creative thinking scores on the Torrance Tests of Creative Thinking." *Creativity Research Journal 23.4* (2011): 285-295. <http://www.creativitypost.com/education/yes_there_is_a_creativity_crisis>.

Linkner, Josh. "How Kids Lose Their Creativity As They Age (And How To Prevent It)." *Forbes* 16 Oct 2014. <https://www.forbes.com/sites/joshlinkner/2014/10/16/how-kids-lose-their-creativity-as-they-age-and-how-to-prevent-it/#3e41d1e0422e>.

Merritt, Jonathan. "The Creativity Crisis." *Q Ideas* (2017).

Myers, Karen K., and Kamyab Sadaghiani. "Millennials in the workplace: A communication perspective on millennials' organizational relationships and performance." *Journal of Business and Psychology 25.2* (2010): 225-238.

National Assembly of State Arts Agencies. "Why should government support the arts." *State Policy Briefs* (2010).

Orr, Greg. "Diffusion of Innovations, by Everett Rogers (1995)." (2003).

Picciuto, Elizabeth, and Peter Carruthers. "The origins of creativity." *The philosophy of creativity: New Essays* (2014): 199-223.

Al Ries and Jack Trout. "Positioning: The Battle For Your Mind." 1981, McGraw-Hill Inc.

Robinson, Ken. "How Schools Kill Creativity." *Creative by Nature* 26 Apr 2015.

Simonton, Dean Keith. *The Psychology of Creativity: A Historical Perspective*. 2001. <https://simonton.faculty.ucdavis.edu/wp-content/uploads/sites/243/2015/08/HistoryCreativity.pdf>.

Solomon, Yoram. "3 Not-So-Surprising Reasons Corporate America Kills Creativity." 2018. *Inc.* 30 Aug 2018. <https://www.inc.com/guadalupe-gonzalez/us-mexico-trade-agreement-nafta-negotiations-what-it-means-for-your-business.html>.

St John, Donna. "Extraordinary and Inevitable Synthesis of Visual Media, Education and Neurological Transformations in 21st Century Pedagogy." (2016).

Westby, Erik L., and V. L. Dawson. "Creativity: Asset or burden in the classroom?" *Creativity Research Journal 8.1* (1995): 1-10.

Woolsey, Taylor. "How Standardized Testing Kills Creativity In Education." n.d. *LivingOut.Social.* 29 Aug 2018. <http://livingout.social/how-standardized-testing-kills-creativity-in-education#>.

Bowers, Brent. "Study Shows Stronger Links Between Entrepreneurs and Dyslexia." The New York Times - Breaking News,

World News & Multimedia, 5 Nov. 2007, www.nytimes.com/2007/12/05/business/worldbusiness/05iht-dyslexia.4.8602036.html.

Eide, Fernette. "Dyslexia | What Are the Super-Powers of Successful Dyslexic Entrepreneurs?" Dyslexia | Dyslexic Advantage, www.dyslexicadvantage.org/dyslexia-famous-dyslexic-entrepreneurs/.

Gladwell, Malcolm. David and Goliath: Underdogs, misfits, and the art of battling giants. Hachette UK, 2013.

Jackson, Joshua K. "How Dyslexia Drives Success in Entrepreneurs." The Codpast, 2 Nov. 2016, thecodpast.org/2015/09/how-dyslexia-drives-success-in-entrepreneurs/.

Singh, H. Ramananda, and Habib Rahman. "Traits of Successful Entrepreneurs KEYWORDS: Entrepreneurial traits, risk." Management 2.11 (2013).

Snyder, Benjamin. "Here Are 5 Business Leaders Who Live With Dyslexia." Fortune, 15 Oct. 2015, fortune.com/2015/10/15/business-leaders-dyslexia/.

Wehbe, Shada. "7 Characteristics of a Successful Business Leader - Potential." The Online Learning Platform, 17 Apr. 2018, www.potential.com/articles/7-characteristics-of-a-successful-business-leader/.

The Guardian, "Dyslexic entrepreneurs-why they have a competitive edge." January 2015, https://www.the guardian.com/small-business-network/2015/jan/15/dyslexic-entreprneurs-competetive-edge-business-leaders

Best, M.L., 2014. The internet that Facebook built. Communications of the ACM, 57(12), pp.21-23.

Denicolai, Stefano, Roger Strange, and Antonella Zucchella. "The dynamics of the outsourcing relationship." The Future Of Global Organizing. Emerald Group Publishing Limited, 2015. 341-364.

Drake Baer. "9 Critical Turning Points That Shaped Mark Cuban's Extraordinary Career"

Business Insider. 3 Nov 2014, https://www.businessinsider.com/mark-cuban-critical-career-decisions-2014-11?IR=T

Eric Rosenbaum. "Musk's 'out of cash' dilemma many business founders love to share." CNBC.

27 April 2017. https://www.cnbc.com/2017/04/27/the-crucial-decision-teslas-elon-musk-had-to-make-when-he-was-broke.html

Irani, Lilly. "Difference and dependence among digital workers: The case of Amazon

Mechanical Turk." *South Atlantic Quarterly* 114.1 (2015): 225-234.

Joel Brown. "The 5 Great Lessons Walt Disney Taught Us." Addicted to Success. 24 September 2012. https://addicted2success.com/success-advice/the-5-great-lessons-walt-disney-taught-us/

Kantor, Jodi, and David Streitfeld. "Inside Amazon: Wrestling big ideas in a bruising workplace." *New York Times* 15 (2015): 74-80.

Lillestol, Tayllor, Dallen J. Timothy, and Rebekka Goodman. "Competitive strategies in the US theme park industry: a popular media perspective." *International Journal of Culture, Tourism and Hospitality Research* 9.3 (2015): 225-240.

Matthews, Charles H., and Ralph Brueggemann. *Innovation and entrepreneurship: A competency framework*. Routledge, 2015. 23-35.

Niphadkar, Chaitanya. "The new age transformational leader: Richard Branson." *International Journal of Scientific & Engineering Research* 8.6 (2017): 542-547.

Parker, Simon C. "Who become serial and portfolio entrepreneurs?" *Small Business Economics* 43.4 (2014): 887-898.

Printed in the United States
By Bookmasters